BUY
YOURSELF
A JOB
&
BE YOUR
OWN
BOSS

ABOUT THE AUTHOR

Graham Cunningham, C.A., is a partner in the firm of G.G. Cunningham & Associates as well as a lecturer at York University in the Entrepreneurial Studies Program. A writer/editor of several business publications, he co-authored a home-learning course for TVOntario, *"Start Your Own Business"*, and contributes to Bank of Montreal's quarterly newsletter, *"Independent Business Review"*. With his interest in seeing that small business owners obtain the necessary financial management support, he has developed professional courses for The Society of Management Accountants of Ontario on *"How To Start a Private Practice,"* and a second on *"How to Manage a Private Practice."*

BUY
YOURSELF
A JOB
&
BE YOUR
OWN
BOSS

Graham Cunningham

McGraw-Hill Ryerson
Montreal   Toronto

First published in 1990 by
McGraw-Hill Ryerson Limited
330 Progress Avenue
Toronto, Canada
M1P 2Z5

Canadian Cataloguing in Publication Data

Cunningham, Graham
  Buy yourself a job and be your own boss

ISBN 0-07-551057-X

1. New business enterprises. 2. Small business —
Management. I. Title.

HD62.5.C85 1990   658.1'1   C90-094184-7

References to income tax apply at the time the book was written.
Please check with your accountant or tax expert as income legisla-
tion is subject to change.

Typesetting: Jay Tee Graphics Ltd.
Printed in Canada

For Florence
Mother of
David, Glenn, Lauri, Rob

ACKNOWLEDGMENTS

I now realize that no book can be published without the support and assistance of many friends and associates. Although it's impossible to mention everyone, I feel some should be recognised.

Don Loney provided continual guidance in developing the outline to the final edit. Editor Darlene Zeleny provided the creative restructuring and improved the book immensely. Tom Gallagher provided invaluable technical input and assistance for the initial draft.

Special thanks to our clients and other small business owners who provided real-life small business experiences that are related throughout the book.

Writing this book would not be possible without the support and expertise of my three original partners in the C.A. firm — Ron Clark, Doug Hodgkinson and Les Solomon. Brenda Bott, our secretary, spent countless hours transcribing and re-transcribing the various chapters and re-edits over a period of six months.

As it was with establishing the business, this book would not be possible without the continued support of my wife Florence.

Last, I would like to thank the person who fired me back in 1971. He provided the opportunity for me to buy myself a job and be my own boss.

CONTENTS

LIST OF EXHIBITS

INTRODUCTION

In June 1971, I heard those devastating two words: "You're fired." My quick reaction was, "Wow, what do I do now?" By the way, "You're fired" was said in the 1970s. Things have changed in the '80s and '90s—you get "dehired" or "early retired." Same result. End of career as general manager of a small marketing company.

As it turns out, over the preceding couple of years I had developed an idea about starting up my own business. After seven agonizing days, there was no doubt in my mind that I would capitalize on this idea. I had the desire and was committed. I had confidence in myself. Most important, the family was on-side. Being fired was a blessing in disguise. It afforded me the opportunity to "buy myself a job," be my own boss, and finance it with my severance allowance.

So, the decision was made, and new excitement entered my life. My idea was to set up my own business and be a part-time controller for five small businesses. I had determined that a reasonable monthly fee would be $500, and that's $30,000 a year. My expenses would be minimal as I planned to work out of my home. My salary at the time was $20,000. What an opportunity. I can buy myself a job, be my own boss, make more money, and no one can fire me.

Now it's twenty years later and G.G. Cunningham and Associates has seven partners and a bright future. Buying myself a job was the best business decision I've ever made.

If you are working for a big company, I suggest that deep down you want to be in your own business. The main reason is to be your own boss. The idea of making your own decisions and being responsible for "calling the shots" will no doubt override the main disadvantage associated with running a small business—no guaranteed paycheques.

This is reinforced by the report from Statistics Canada which showed that, between 1975 and 1986, the number of self-employed workers in the country increased more than twice as fast as did the number of paid workers. Women and older workers spearheaded this movement toward self-employment.

The growth of small business is a sign of the times. The 1980s highlighted the "era of the entrepreneur." The long-term driving force of the economy will be spearheaded by this group. The 1980s have also seen the effects of the re-structuring of the world economy. It spelt the end of the industrial smoke-stack era. Alvin Toffler, in his book *The Third Wave*, presents this theory: The first wave was the agricultural revolution which began about 9,000 BC, and about 300 years ago, the second wave, called the industrial revolution began. The industrial revolution saw the immigration of farmers to the industrialized urban areas. Today, we are well into the third wave, "the information society."

One of Alvin Toffler's key words is *demassification*. During the 1980s, the buzz words were *dehiring, downsizing*, and *early retirements*. The big corporations eliminated many layers of management. This provided a flattening effect to the management pyramid between the ultimate decision-makers and the doers. The bigger corporations' downsizing includes blue-collar workers, who are sometimes referred to as "techno peasants," and office workers. But mergers and automation trends will no doubt accelerate in the 1990s. This will provide a great opportunity for many Canadians to buy themselves a job and be their own bosses.

In the United States, nearly 500,000 corporate executives, administrators, and managers lost their jobs between 1981 and 1985. I have no statistics on the loss of blue-collar and general office-staff jobs. I suggest that they are much higher. Since then, the number can only have grown, given the corporate mergers and acquisitions, and the downsizing by large companies. This would suggest that the number for Canada is 50,000. However, unconfirmed reports in the early 1980s indicated that the displaced executives numbered about 150,000.

The late 1980s have seen many leveraged buyouts and mergers of major corporations. The ultimate effect is a reduction in employment in the consolidated groups. The army of those dehired, retired, or downsized will accelerate in the 1990s.

The main advantage of this group is that their basic skills have been developed. Some have reached a mature point in their lives and probably accumulated some personal assets in the form of a home or investments and they no doubt also received reasonable compensation on their departure from a big corporation. This equity capital combined with their skills and general knowledge can provide a good base upon which to start a new business.

This book is primarily directed to individuals who have joined the ranks of the downsized, dehired, or retired, and to presently employed middle managers who wish to consider a career alternative to that of employee to employer. This book will also be of interest to students in the Entrepreneurial Studies Programs in the colleges and universities across Canada who have made the decision to be their own bosses.

Buy Yourself a Job means just that. You will be required to take some of your earnings, your life savings, and investments to invest in a start-up, the purchase of a business or the purchase of a franchise to take advantage of the career alternative and buy yourself a job.

In reading this book, you can expect to examine yourself and determine what you really want out of life. You will understand what makes entrepreneurs tick, and how they arrive at the ideas that motivate them to start their own businesses. The ins and outs of buying a business and the advantages and disadvantages of a franchise are discussed thoroughly. Conducting a feasibility study to determine whether the new venture can survive and provide you with a reasonable lifestyle is probably the most important step to take before your hard-earned savings are spent. The preparation of a simple business plan is dealt with as a follow-up from the feasibility study so you will know the cash requirements for a successful start-up.

If it is still a go, then I will discuss the legal aspects of whether you should incorporate or operate as a sole proprietorship. In addition, I discuss in detail what I refer to as the management tripod. The three legs consist of marketing (get the business), operations (do the business), and finance (make a reasonable profit). Now that you are in operation, profit planning becomes essential and this is spearheaded by how you price your products or services to provide the optimum profit. You will no doubt consider computerizing your operation from the outset, if only to handle your correspondence through word processing.

Once you have been in business for a while, you will be interested in the detailed discussion on staying in business and in handling your personal financial affairs.

Finally, I will deal with reassessing personal and business goals, and help determine the degree of growth required to meet your personal goals.

1

WHO YOU ARE

During the recession of the early 1980s, the federal government began to realize the importance of small companies. Research studies indicated that in both Canada and the United States small businesses are the major job creators. Mergers, automation, and downsizing made the bigger corporations negative employers. So, during the 1980s, government assistance to small business increased dramatically. (See Exhibit 1.)

EXHIBIT 1

JOB CREATION IN CANADA 1978-1986
TOTAL NET CHANGE IN JOBS

Number of Employees in Company	Increase Change
Less than 5	53%
5-19	22%
20-49	7%
50-99	3%
100+	15%

The Annual Report on Small Business in Ontario: The State of Small Business, 1988.

   This is evidenced by changes in the federal budgets during the 1980s that include the following: Capital gains exemption—up to $500,000 on the sale of the shares of Canadian-controlled private corporations (small businesses); spousal salary deductible for proprietorships; gift and death taxes eliminated; taxpayer innocent until proven guilty (prior to this, a taxpayer in a dispute with the government was forced to pay the tax before discussion); Small Business Loans' Act limit increased to $100,000; major reduction in paperwork for small business; RRSP investment in small business (not practical but was an effort); and the reversal of the dividend distribution tax. Some provinces implemented income-tax holidays and equity-financing vehicles to support small business.

   Changes in the educational system have also been happening. Until the late 1970s, the educational system—secondary schools, universities and colleges—had done little to encourage entrepreneurship by placing emphasis on training young people to be employees. Too much of the student's learning emphasized finding a job or adapting to a job, rather than developing the skills, confidence, and experience that would allow youth to create their own jobs, or at least present an alternative career path.

   In contrast, the 1980s saw a tremendous increase in activity in the educational area. Many colleges and universities in Canada developed entrepreneurial or small-business educational programs. The Ontario government, for example, established a curriculum for the secondary schools. In addition, they funded six entrepreneurial centers in Ontario. So, now the federal and provincial governments and the educational systems in Canada are providing support to the small-business or entrepreneurial sector. Most Canadians are now aware that they can start their own businesses, be entrepreneurs, and be their own bosses.

   What, then, is an entrepreneur? In my view, all of the definitions can be summarized by the one in the Oxford dictionary: "A person in effective control of a commercial undertaking." The key words are "effective control." Tom Peters, while researching his book *In Search of Excellence*, observed that time and again extraordinary energy was exerted by frontline workers when given a modicum of apparent control. In other words, the ability to work on their own and have some control over what happened in an entrepreneurial environment, greatly improved their performance. He cites the example of two groups who were put into two different rooms to handle identical problems, namely complex puzzles and a proofreading chore. Annoying noises were piped into both rooms during the performance of these tasks. The only difference was that in one room, the individuals were informed that there was an off button available to them if they wished it. On completion of the task, the group who had access to the off button solved five times the number of puzzles and made only a tiny number of proofreading errors. The group with the off button did not actually use it, but they did have a feeling of control over their environment.

Individuals, regardless of their personality and background, can learn how to get "effective control" to start up an entrepreneurial activity and join the group spearheading the future of the Canadian economy.

The Importance of Goal Setting

First and foremost, before you even consider buying yourself a job, you must take a hard look at yourself and determine what you really want to be doing. In simple terms, you need to set your personal and business goals. Goals add purpose and lend direction to life. Without goals, we drift. It is essential to have goals at all stages of our lives: for school, career, and retirement. A cavalier attitude will result in a lower level of personal and business success. Goal setting should be part of the individual's personal lifetime plan. As a by-product, goal setting will relieve some of the stress caused by uncertainty. Setting goals is the first step in making things happen, whether in your personal or business life. If you are an employee and you cannot reach your goals in your present position, then you may wish to consider an alternative course. Personal goal setting is a prerequisite of personal growth, self-improvement, and success. As we will discuss in later chapters, the driving force of any business will be goal setting and good planning to achieve these goals.

How do you go about setting goals for yourself? Initially, reflect on what you really want out of life. Do a self-analysis by listing everything you can think of that you would like to see happen in your lifetime. Some of the individual goals may be in conflict, so it is important to prioritize the individual goals. For example, your career goal may be to start your own business whereas a personal goal may be to spend more time with your family. This can be a conflict.

If it cannot be expressed in writing, it is unlikely that it can be achieved. Be specific. Don't say you want to own your own business; state a specific goal, such as: "I want to establish a small business in the retail clothing area that will have annual sales of $1,000,000 by January 1995." Each goal must be realistic, have a specific time frame, and be quantitative. By the way, the time frame is not tomorrow. Similarly, when you set up your own business, you should have adequate lead time, whether it is six months, a year, or two years to develop the plan, acquire the necessary skills, and the capital. One of the major problems with the downsized, dehired, early retired big-business middle managers is that they tend to jump at the first apparent opportunity and do not take the time to examine their personal goals and plan the start-up using a reasonable time frame. These account for the many failures in the first five years. As W.C. Fields once said, "Patience, my boy."

Getting caught up in the entrepreneurial wave can be a complete disaster for some aspiring entrepreneurs. Although entrepreneurism is a science and not an art, it can be difficult for some big-company executives to make the transition from corporate office to small-business owner. When you buy yourself a job, you must wear many hats. You don't have a secretary to perform many of the tasks that you took for granted in the past. As a business owner, you make the major decisions personally, not by committee. You can move very quickly unlike the slow decisions of a big business. You must become a generalist, whereas in big business, you were probably a specialist. Make one big mistake in a small business, and there is no business, whereas big business usually has financial depth and can sustain a major mistake. You will be a doer. Big-business executives play politics. If you fail, you can lose everything, including all your personal assets. If a big-business manager fails, he or she receives the golden handshake in the form of six-months'-to-a-year's salary and other benefits. So, before anyone makes the move from the big corporate office to the small-business desk, it is important to recognize the difference in the two positions. The major difference is that management is a job, whereas ownership is a way of thinking, an attitude.

You become a long-term planner with ultimate retirement in sight. Your plans deal with a vision for the long term. Big-company corporate executives are more concerned about quarterly results and this year's bonus. Their thinking must often be short term.

Before you make the move to buy yourself a job, you must know your weaknesses. To get "effective control," you should perform a personal analysis. You should consider your small business as a hat on your head. You are sitting on a three-legged stool. You are the key but your business will only be as strong as the weakest leg of the stool. I refer to the stool as the management tripod. Each of the legs of the tripod represent one major management area. The first is marketing. (Get the business.) The second is operations. (Do the business.) The third is finance. (Make a reasonable profit.) The strength of your business will be determined by the weakest leg. General analysis of small-business owners indicates that most know how to do the business (operation's leg). Their second strength is marketing, and their weakest leg is finance.

The Federal Business Development Bank has established a simple questionnaire that will help you to determine your strengths and weaknesses objectively. This analysis has nothing to do with your personality. You cannot fail this test. The main purpose is to determine weak areas. The next step is to correct your weaknesses with seminars, management textbooks, outside consultants, partners, or senior employees. (See Exhibit 2.) This will be the basis of your start-up plan.

Up to this point, I have referred to the middle managers who find themselves part of the economic restructuring of the business world. I would now like to draw attention to

EXHIBIT 2

ASSESS YOUR STRENGTHS

Self-Assessment
1. I have specific personal goals in writing, complete with target dates. _____
2. I always plan before starting anything. _____
3. I enjoy putting my ideas into practice. _____
4. I like to take charge and make things happen. _____
5. I can evaluate alternatives, make sound decisions, and resolve problems effectively. _____
6. I am in good physical health and able to cope with stress. _____
7. I have built up a good circle of business contacts. _____
8. My spouse and/or family support my new venture 100 percent. _____
9. I am confident in my ability to meet targets. _____
10. I can work hard for long hours. _____

Marketing Leg
1. I know how to conduct a market-research study and interpret the results. _____
2. I have experience in developing advertising and promotional programs. _____
3. I am familiar with the various sales-distribution channels. _____
4. I am familiar with the operation of a sales force. _____
5. I know how to identify customers and approach them to make a sale. _____
6. I have experience in customer relations and the handling of complaints. _____
7. I know how to price a product/service for a maximum profit. _____
8. I have experience in getting publicity, preparing news releases, and creating a good image. _____

9. I know how to evaluate competition. _____
10. I know how to monitor the marketing activity. _____

Operations Leg
1. I have experience in supervising people. _____
2. I have developed effective listening skills. _____
3. I have experience in hiring subordinates, assessing performance, and motivating employees. _____
4. I understand the need for continuing research and product development. _____
5. I know how to choose suppliers and negotiate the best price and terms when purchasing products/services. _____
6. I have experience in the techniques of inventory control. _____
7. I have experience in negotiating leases. _____
8. I am experienced in the use of computers. _____
9. I am familiar with employee-benefit programs. _____
10. I am familiar with all types of general insurance. _____

Finance Leg
1. I am familiar with the various sources of financing. _____
2. I am familiar with bookkeeping procedures and can interpret financial statements. _____
3. I have experience in preparing profit and loss and cash flow forecasts. _____
4. I have experience in developing credit policies and collecting accounts receivable. _____
5. I recognize the need for outside financial support — accountant, banker and lawyer. _____
6. I have a good credit rating. _____
7. I have experience in developing business plans. _____
8. I have access to adequate financial resources to start and operate a small business. _____
9. I am familiar with the various government programs. _____
10. I recognize the need for current accurate information to monitor my business. _____

the young, aspiring entrepreneurs who are in universities. It is interesting to note that the majority of people starting new small businesses have post-secondary degrees. (See Exhibit 3.) Since 1980, I have been teaching in the entrepreneurial studies program in the Business School at York University, Toronto. Most of the students in this program aspire to have their own businesses. Many graduating from the Business School are anxious to commence immediately without obtaining the necessary first-hand business experience and without establishing the network of associates that will be required for the ultimate success of the enterprise. On a positive note, I am familiar with several who have started up and are operating very successful small-business enterprises. However, I feel that these are the exception.

EXHIBIT 3

WHO ARE THE ENTREPRENEURS
— BY EDUCATION

Less than secondary school 32.6%
Secondary-school diploma 10.6%
Post-secondary 56.7%

(Statistics Canada)

My advice to them has always been: "Get a job with a big corporation and be trained in the business world." As Peter Drucker indicated in an interview published in *Inc.* (a U.S. small-business publication): "The most successful of the young entrepreneurs today are people who have spent five to eight years in a big business organization." He goes on to say: "They get tools. They learn how to do a cashflow analysis and how one trains people; how one delegates; and how one builds a team. The ones without that background are the entrepreneurs who, no matter how great their success, are being pushed out." He then refers to Mr. Jobs of the sensationally successful Apple Computer Inc. He goes on to say, "Without this five to ten years of management under your belts before you start, you can make some 'asinine mistakes.' " And remember, in small business one major mistake can be its demise.

If your personal goals suggest that you should be in your own business and you have prepared a plan to offset your weak areas, then you can advance to the next step. There are four parts to this step. 1. You must have a good idea (product or service); 2. You must have the desire (commitment); 3. You must have faith (confidence); and 4. You must have the support of your family. We will discuss how you might develop an idea for a product or service in detail in Chapter 2.

My Idea

I commenced my business July 1, 1971. My idea was developed during my tenure as the general manager of a small marketing business. My job was to set up and service dealers throughout the United States, Canada, and abroad. The product was a teaching aid for all levels of education. Virtually all of the dealers were owner managed. I became aware very quickly that these dealers had virtually no financial-management skills. I would spend more time discussing their financial affairs than the marketing of our product. After two and one-half years, the thought occurred to me that there was room for a part-time controller service for small-business owners who lacked the financial skills necessary to optimize the success of their businesses. In other words, I could provide the outside service to support the finance leg of the dealer's management tripod. The thought of going it alone is pretty scary. As one entrepreneur wrote: "Welcome to the club of terror." The main terror is: Can I survive financially?

Desire and Faith

Before the starting date, I read a book called *Think and Grow Rich*. This book is now available on audio tapes. I suggest that everyone considering buying a job should either read the book or listen to the tapes. The prevalent words in the book are desire (commitment) and faith (confidence). If you do not have a strong personal desire and faith in your product or service, then you won't succeed.

Desire or commitment are simple words. But these can be the key words to enhance the terror in starting. The key phrase is "burn your bridges." In this manner, there is only one method of survival, and that is to succeed: no alternative, no backstop, no turning back, totally committed. This may sound foreign to many who suggest that you should start a business on the side and work into it. If you are doing this, you are not committed and the long-term success is in doubt. On the other hand, I do not suggest that you start a business until the planning has been done. These details will be covered in future chapters. This is reinforced by the story of the ancient warriors who traveled by ship to the enemy shores. On arrival, they discovered that they were outnumbered ten to one. The immediate thought was to retreat in their boats back home. The leader burned the ships. There was only one way to go. That's commitment. And, yes, they won.

Whatever your product or service, you must have faith or confidence in the quality and your ability to market, deliver, and make a reasonable profit. Be a strong, positive thinker and have faith that you can do it. This does not mean blind faith. You must have the skills.

In the pre-start-up stage, do yourself a favor. When you wake up, get up. Even at 4:00 AM. Don't let some of the insecure thoughts take over your mind while you are dozing in the morning. Get up, get a paper and pencil, and start making notes on the pros and cons of your new venture.

Your self-confidence can be supported by developing a network of business associates who can help you in your new business and provide input to cover your weak areas.

Without realizing it, you probably developed contacts or business-association friends whom you can call on from time to time for input, support, and general discussion. In my case, I was thirty-nine when I started the business. I developed a network of business associates and friends who had marketing and operations skills that complemented my skills in the financial area. In the early stages of my business, I found the network invaluable. The network provided the outside, objective support that I needed.

That old expression, "It's lonely at the top," is very prevalent when you start a business on your own with no partners or senior staff. It's a good idea to make a list of individuals that you have dealt with over the years. Then determine what area of assistance they might provide for your new business. Some might suggest that using your friends and colleagues in this manner is not proper. This is not the case. Your network colleagues are pleased to be of any assistance. Remember, it's a two-way street and you will find yourself on the giving end of your network system. The main thing to keep in mind is to take advantage of all the resources that are available so that your business can be successful.

Family

All of the above means nothing if you do not have the 100-percent support of your family. My wife, Florence, provided the major support and allowed me to pursue the necessary hours and off-hours that were required to set the foundation for the company. This played a major role. I was able to concentrate totally on getting the business going with little concern about the state of affairs of the household; they were in good hands.

Statistics Canada indicates that more than 40% of the new businesses in the 1980s were started by individuals over the age of 45. (See Exhibit 4.) With the increase in longevity in our time, a 40-year-old is probably about halfway through his or her lifetime. To end Chapter 1, I would like to emphasize the point that you are never too old to buy yourself a job.

If you have ever aspired to be your own boss, then the worst thing that can happen is to wake up when you are over 65 years old and say, "I never tried."

EXHIBIT 4

WHO ARE THE ENTREPRENEURS — BY AGE

Under 24 . . . .   4.5%
25–34 . . . . 23.7%
35–44 . . . . 31.4%
45–54 . . . . 22.5%
55–64 . . . . 13.8%
Over 65 . . . .   4.2%

(Statistics Canada)

2

STARTING FROM SCRATCH: WHAT YOU NEED TO KNOW

As a banker once said, "Ideas are a dime a dozen." The point here is simple. Good ideas are worthless if you cannot turn them into a successful commercial venture. In other words, the idea must be marketable at a price that will pay the operating costs and provide a reasonable return on the investment within a few years. And if you ever needed proof of how hard that task can be, ask some of the big companies who introduce numerous products every year and discover that eight out of ten fail.

So, how do you go about dreaming up a great idea to start your own business? Well, before you spend the time and sleepless nights staring at the ceiling and racking your brain for "the idea," you should consider the alternative methods of getting into your own business. There are three possible ways:

1. Start from scratch
2. Buy a business
3. Buy a franchise.

This chapter will focus on starting from scratch. Chapter 4 will deal with buying a business or franchise.

Getting Ideas

Let's assume that you wish to start from scratch and so develop your own idea. The key is the ability to recognize opportunity. Simple ideas from ordinary sources can be the chief motivator. Some of the ordinary sources can be developed at work, be a continual annoyance, a necessity, or hobbies.

Many individuals working for big companies at the present time should consider investigating or reviewing the various activities of the company. Areas that appear to be insignificant to a large business may be a very worthwhile idea or niche for establishing your own business. No doubt, ideas can be generated by "bull sessions" with your friends and business associates. Small business is "niche" marketing, and these are generally areas where the big-business counterparts are really not interested. An example is an individual who was working for a big company that supplied a product to the building trade. He observed that there was an upcoming market for adhesives for PVC piping. This was a "niche" market of about $2,000,000 in Canada. The basic supplier was another large international company. This was a comparatively insignificant market for the big company. Recognizing this as an opportunity, he started his own business, virtually in his garage. The owner was able literally to prepare the adhesive substance in barrels in his garage. He prepared sales literature and packaging materials and sold the product directly to the distributors who supplied mechanical contractors and plumbers. Within five years, he had fifty percent of the market or about $1,000,000 in sales and was earning more than reasonable profits. This idea was generated through working for his previous employer.

The original idea for starting my business was similar. I came to realize that outside accountants (or public accountants) were not providing the financial services required by small-business owners. My idea was to provide small-business owners who could not afford a full-time controller with part-time controller and part-time vice-president of finance services.

Other ideas come from a personal annoyance. For example, Alex Tilley, an avid yachtsman, was continually frustrated by the fact that every hat he purchased would blow off his head, fall in the water, and sink. His idea was to make a hat that wouldn't blow off and if it did, it would float. That was the original idea for the Tilley Endurables hat. From a standing start in 1984, Mr. Tilley saw the expansion of the hat into a full line of clothing for the outdoors. His creative ads in the daily newspapers and other publications have made the "Tilley Endurables" name a household word for quality and style. All of this resulted from the simple annoyance of losing his hat while yachting.

Other ideas have been generated by the sheer necessity of earning income. Greig Clark, while in university, discovered that he needed a summer job to finance the following year's educational expenses, but the best-paying job available did not satisfy his financial needs for the following year. He had heard that other university students had started their own painting businesses, and that it was essentially a simple project with a lot of hard work. He estimated that this project would earn enough to finance the following year's education. In the second year, he hired additional helpers, and his net earnings were well in excess of his educational requirements. During this time, he discovered that most of the painting firms that were unionized did little residential work. It was now obvious that students could earn better-than-average salaries in the summer by using his format. A combination of the requirements of students to earn a reasonable amount during the summer months and the fact that professional painters were not attacking the residential market was the basis for establishing the successful franchise, College Pro Painters.

Hobbies can also generate ideas. For example, Rene Unger is an excellent cook and has been making her own salad dressings for years. She would always make more than she could use and would give the excess to friends. She spent months researching the venture and, lo and behold, Rene's Gourmet Products was formed. Other hobbies in photography, stamp collecting, knitting, sketching or cartooning, painting, and so forth can be hobbies converted into entrepreneurial projects.

Ideas are available in various newspaper articles and trade

magazines. It is sometimes worthwhile to visit trade shows and pay particular attention to new fads on the horizon.

If you have a strong desire to be in your own business and no ideas develop from necessity, annoyance, work, or hobbies, then you will have to take the time to create a new idea. It is quite possible that the idea for your new business may be in an area where you have no previous experience. There are many cases of successful start-ups that took place in areas where the owner did not have experience, but took the time to research the market and took the necessary courses and/or read books to develop the expertise necessary for the successful business.

Choosing a Sector

If you know exactly what it is you want to do—for example, manufacture a new line of toys or open a sporting-goods store—you will automatically place yourself at a particular level of the marketing chain or in a particular sector. If you're not sure or don't have a well-developed idea, you might start by thinking about the *sector* you'd like to be involved in.

There are five sectors: manufacturing, manufacturer's rep or broker, wholesaler, retailer, and service. The manufacturer's rep and the service sectors are generally the easiest to start up and the least costly. Service industries that deal directly with the customer—for example, dry-cleaning stores, travel agents, financial services, consulting services, restaurants, advertising specialties, data-processing services, and so forth—constitute a separate sector. Manufacturing can be considered the most difficult and the most costly in terms of investment. The degree of difficulty and the financial requirements for retailers and wholesalers is in the middle.

Once you have decided on the sector, you must determine the feasibility of the whole project. This will be discussed in Chapter 3.

Let us now look at the pros and cons of the various sectors.

Manufacturing Sector

This is the most difficult to start up. You not only require a product that can be a successful commercial venture, but you need the equipment necessary to manufacture the product, the expertise in the manufacturing process, and an adequate facility that will house the equipment and provide for some reasonable expansion. In other words, you will require more expertise and more financial support to start up in this sector.

In addition to the upfront financing required for equipment and leasehold improvements to the manufacturing facility, additional financing is required for working capital. The business cycle in the manufacturing concern is much longer than in any other sector. The business cycle is the number of days it takes for the money expended for inventory to be recouped on the sale of the product through accounts receivable (in other words, the number of days of accounts receivable plus inventory minus the number of days of accounts payable). The number of days of inventory is determined by the lead time necessary between purchasing the raw material, manufacturing or processing this material into a finished product, and shipping it to the customer. In many cases, manufacturers require three months of inventory of raw materials, work-in-progress, and finished goods in order to provide timely shipments to their customers. Although every industry is different, you can expect that you will require about 90 days of inventory (raw material, work in progress, and finished goods), upwards of 60 days of accounts receivable, less accounts payable of, say, 60 days, for a business cycle of 90 days. Consequently, the manufacturing sector is not only more risky than the others, but it is also more costly to start up and requires more financing after start-up and expansion.

Manufacturers' Rep or Broker

This is the simplest manner of starting up your own business. Manufacturers' reps or brokers act as sales agents for manufacturers. They normally sell manufacturers' products to wholesalers or directly to retailers and receive a percentage of the selling price as their remuneration. Merchandise is shipped directly from the manufacturer to the wholesaler or retailer so the broker will have no accounts receivable or accounts payable pertaining to these products.

The start-up investment is minimal. You are only required

to finance your personal lifestyle. Normally you are paid commission on the sales of one month by the end of the following month.

The major start-up problem is to obtain adequate product lines that will provide you with commissions to sustain your lifestyle. In most cases, you will be responsible for your own expenses.

Wholesale Sector

Starting up a wholesale business does not require the same amount of capital as a manufacturing concern. You will require a warehouse facility, but you will not need any manufacturing equipment, and the costs of leasehold improvements for electrical power and so forth are much less. The amount of inventory on hand varies dramatically by industry, but it is fair to assume that an average would be between 60 and 90 days. The accounts receivable could be upwards to 60 days, the accounts payable could be 60 days, and so the business cycle would be between 60 and 90 days. This should be about 30 days less than the manufacturing concern. One of the major problems with wholesalers is the lack of adequate inventory control. They suffer from the consequences of Pareto's Law which suggests that 20% of inventory accounts for 80% of sales. Poor inventory control can result in an increased business cycle and tie up much needed cash to finance the business.

As the wholesale company expands, the business cycle will remain the same, but the actual cash required to finance the expansion can be substantial. This is dealt with in Chapter 10.

The main advantage, however, is that there are no manufacturing problems, and you are mainly concerned with marketing the manufacturer's products, maintaining adequate inventory control, and providing delivery service to the retailer.

It is important to note that the gross profit for wholesalers varies dramatically by industry. For example, wholesale tobacco has an average of about 10% to 12%, floor coverings 25% to 27%, hardware 30% to 32%. The respective trade associations will, no doubt, have statistics on these and other financial aspects of particular industries. However, the Robert Morris Associates statistics that are compiled annually in the United States will also provide a yardstick as to the gross profit percentage realized by the various wholesale industries.

Retail Sector

The retail sector is the vendor to the ultimate consumer. Although it may require substantial upfront financing for fixtures, leasehold improvements, and inventory, the initial capital would no doubt be less than what is needed for a manufacturing operation. The business cycle is shorter than in either the wholesale or the manufacturing sector. There should be no accounts receivable other than credit cards. (Visa and MasterCard are banked the same day, but American Express can take a week or so for payment.) Inventory should be in the area of 60 to 90 days. Accounts payable can be anywhere up to 60 days, so the business cycle is about 30 days. The gross profit for retailers varies dramatically. For example, clothing usually brings in a profit of about 40%; building materials, 25%; general merchandise, 25%; convenience stores, 23%; jewelry stores, 45%; and so forth. It is, therefore, important to determine a reasonable yardstick for the gross profit of the industry that you have selected. We will discuss this later.

Service Sector

Most industries in the service sector require minimal investment in fixed assets at the start-up. For example, a consulting business can be started from the home, a travel agency requires some furniture (which can be leased). However, the up-front investment for a restaurant, dry-cleaning plant, or data-processing service can be substantial. One main advantage of the service sector is there is either no or very little inventory and the business cycle is mainly accounts receivable. In the food-service industry, it is possible to purchase the food, sell it, and collect the money before the original product must be paid for. Some industries in the service sector are similar to retailers, and the accounts receivable will be negligible; for example, dry cleaners and restaurants.

However, some in the service sector—for example, advertising specialties, consulting services, and data-processing services—may find they are billing their customers and receiving the cash in, say, 45 to 60 days. Their business cycle is, therefore, 45 to 60 days less any accounts payable that could be offset against this amount. In many cases, the accounts payable are minimal because most of the expenditures are for rent and wages and items that must be paid currently.

The main concern in starting up a retail operation is obtaining the proper location. It has been said many times that the three most important things in a retail operation are location, location, and location. We shall discuss this in detail in Chapter 5.

Other Considerations

In addition to the financial considerations of the various sectors, it is also important to realize that the ultimate pay day in starting up your own business is when you sell. Starting up a manufacturer's rep or broker's business may involve the simplest and least expensive start-up, but it will render the lowest selling price. An exception to this may be if you develop a reasonably large organization with several partners who are prepared to purchase your shares on retirement. But, generally speaking, this type of operation is essentially personal and, without the person, the operation may have little or no value.

The retail and wholesale sectors will attract a selling price usually based on the operation's profitability. In other words, the higher the profit, the higher the selling price. Details of valuation will be dealt with in Chapter 4. This means that the selling price will be higher than the manufacturer's rep or broker, depending of course on the amount of the profits.

The manufacturing sector will render the best selling price in relation to profits. Although it is more difficult to start up, an operation in the manufacturing sector has more substance or assets and, in some cases, may own some patents that would have a value of their own.

If your personal goals suggest that you ultimately want to establish a manufacturing company, but you cannot get adequate financing at the outset, then you may wish to phase in via one of the other sectors. This could be considered the thin edge of the wedge. You can establish yourself in the industry as a manufacturer's rep, explore a broader range of products and, at the right time, plan a start-up manufacturing operation, say in five years. Remember, goal setting at the outset is the prime tool for your ultimate personal success.

The Start-Up

On the surface, starting your own business from scratch can appear to be a reasonably inexpensive approach to being your own boss, and in some cases, it is. However, the long-term success rate of new start-ups is about twenty in one hundred.

So it may be a less expensive way to start up than buying a business or a franchise, but it can be a disaster if proper planning is not in place. The three secrets to a successful start-up are planning, planning, and planning. In other words, you are not going to start off tomorrow. In Chapter 6, we will be showing you how to establish a business plan for a start-up. After you have prepared a business plan together with the necessary forecasts of income, expenses, and cash flow, you may find that your venture is a candidate for the 80% category of failures. Time spent on this planning can be the best investment you will ever make if you wish to be a true entrepreneur.

The importance of planning for a successful start-up is not just a monetary consideration. Yes, you might lose your home and your life savings to date, but an even bigger loss can be the potential disruption of family relations and the personal loss of ego. With the severe consequence of failure, you don't start a business by taking unnecessary chances or any chance for that matter. Become a true entrepreneur and get control—plan, research, and make a calculated risk. As John Paul Getty, touted to be the richest man in the world a few decades ago, once said when asked if he gambled to become so rich: "If I gambled, I made sure I was the house." Make sure you're the house.

You have no doubt read many times that some suggest that in order to be successful, you must fail a few times in order to gain that keen knowledge. This is nonsense. No one should start up a new enterprise with the thought that it might go under and that's part of being an entrepreneur. A true entrepreneur will not fail, and the key to the success will be planning.

The New Company Syndrome

Two other items can be considered harassment to an individual starting up a new business. The first is the New Company Syndrome. This is something that I discovered when I started my business. When you start from scratch, you have no track record. In my case, the upfront investment was minimal. Therefore, my personal investment and potential loss was virtually zero. So, what is the New Company Syndrome? Well, before I commenced business, my enthusiasm suggested that the business would flow in. The fact is, some did or I wouldn't be around. However, it did not happen as fast as I expected. My network of business associates and friends were not, as I expected, running around on my behalf to drum up business. However, some of these individuals realized that I was starting with virtually no monetary commitment and was perhaps lacking in some general experience. I had no track record other than being corporate secretary of a big business and general manager and controller of a small business. There was concern, I am sure, that I might fold up business in six months and go back to being an employee. This resulted in a slow start-up, and my enthusiasm started to wane in the fourth month.

After nine months, a friend/client took me to lunch to ask me if I was going to make it. His concern was what to do if I packed it in. At that point, I realized that there was such a thing as the New Company Syndrome. This would plague other individuals starting from scratch whose friends and acquaintances would have the same concerns. If you are providing a product, whether as a manufacturer, wholesaler, or retailer, and your friend has been receiving good service from a competitor, there is no good reason from a sound business perspective why he should change if there is any thought that you might not be in business in the long term.

I have noticed this with several clients whom I've helped

start up new businesses. In one case, a client was leaving his present big company and starting up a competitive business as a supplier to the graphics industry. During the preparation of the income-statement forecast, I had vigorous discussions regarding the optimistic sales forecast that he was preparing. His enthusiasm and the fact that many of his present customers indicated that they would buy from him when he was on his own resulted in a very unrealistic forecast. He was able to convince the bank that these excessive sales would be forthcoming and received the necessary financing. Within six months after commencement, the actual sales were about 20% of the forecast. The company was in a very tight cash bind, and he was forced to take in a partner and give up more than 50% of the business. The message is clear. Don't be overenthusiastic when preparing the forecast for your start-up business and remember the New Company Syndrome.

Murphy's Law

Another annoyance to a start-up is Murphy's Law. Everybody knows Murphy's Law: "If something can go wrong, it will." You can be sure this is prevalent in a start-up. All of the planning that you will do at the front end will not necessarily cover all of the bases. In one case, an individual started up a business, prepared a business plan which included a forecast of sales and expenses and a forecast cash-flow statement by months. The financing, equipment, and most of the personnel were in place. So what could go wrong? Well, the supplier of the basic material needed for processing delayed shipment for about three months. When the material was received and the shipments made, one of the major customers proved to be bad and the company sustained a sizable bad-debt loss. Six months later, he joined the eighty percent club. There is probably no protection against Murphy's Law, but dedicated, thorough research and planning will go a long way toward minimizing the consequences of being "caught off guard."

3

FORMS OF BUSINESS OWNERSHIP

Now that you have decided to buy yourself a job, it is time to be your own boss. You are the general manager, the vice-president of human resources, the vice-president of finance, and the vice-president of operations. In the past, you either had assistance or staff who specialized in the various areas of the big company. Well, "Them days is gone forever" until your company grows to the point where you can afford this luxury. You are it. Decisions are no longer made by a committee. You make them. However, it is a good idea to bounce major decisions off your network of key business associates that you established before you started up.

One of your first major decisions in starting up your own business is to determine what vehicle you wish to use for your endeavor. By that I mean: Should you start as a proprietorship or incorporate the company?

To Incorporate or Not to Incorporate
The simple approach is to operate as a propietorship and register a company for a nominal amount. This means the business is an extension of yourself. In other words, the company is you. Like anything else, there are advantages and disadvantages. For example, a proprietorship is easy and inexpensive to set up. You are only required to file your personal tax return with a copy of the business financial information on your annual tax return. As assets increase in the busi-

ness, they will be for your personal account. If in your first start-up months there are losses, these losses can be used to offset any other taxable income that you may have earned in the taxation year. Now, for the bad news. You will be personally responsible for any liabilities or debts incurred by the business. This means that if the company fails, all liabilities to third parties, particularly suppliers, will be for your personal account. These third parties will be looking to you personally for payment. Also, if the type of business you are starting has some degree of risk to third parties, then any contingent liabilities sustained will be personal. This means that if you start a restaurant, you are personally liable for any food poisoning. If you commence a delivery business and an accident occurs where the liability is beyond the insurance coverage, then you will be personally liable.

An incorporated company is different. It is a separate legal entity or another person. Any debts incurred by this legal person are for the legal person's account. On failure, the suppliers are looking to the company, not to you personally for payment of any outstanding invoices. Any lawsuits arising from third parties would be for the account of the incorporated company, not you personally.

There are other advantages to incorporation. The legal company will continue in the event of the death of the shareholder or the sale of shares by the shareholder. The disadvantages are that it costs $1,000 or so to incorporate, and you must file two additional income tax returns, one to the federal and one to the provincial governments.

Sole Proprietorship Versus Incorporation

Tax Implications

If you are concerned about third-party liability, then by all means incorporate from the outset. If not, let's look at some income-tax considerations. If you operate as a proprietorship, then the income is for your own account and the profits of the company will be taxed at your personal tax rate. The small business tax rate for an incorporated company is about 22% for the first $200,000 of profit. The federal personal income tax rate for earnings over $55,000 per year is 29% plus the respective provincial tax rate which brings the total rate to about 44%. (This varies with each province.) If you expect your business to be earning in excess of $55,000 before you are paid any remuneration, then you will be paying personal income taxes on income over $55,000 at the 44% rate.

Another question: Will you need all of the company earnings personally? If so, then it makes no sense to incorporate for tax purposes. When the profits through dividends or salary or bonus are passed on to you, the effective income tax will be the same, whether you are incorporated or not. However, if you anticipate some expansion where funds will be required to be retained in the business to finance accounts receivable, inventory, and possibly the purchase of future fixed assets, then you should consider incorporating because these funds can be retained in the business at the lower tax rate of 22%.

Case Studies

An example of the effect that tax can have on your operation can be demonstrated by one of my clients. His business was a sole proprietorship earning about $25,000 per year. The owner used all of the profits to pay for personal expenses. In other words, all of the profits were taken out of the company by the owner. Expansion was minimal, and no funds were required to finance future operations. Happily, the small business owner had monthly financial reports that informed him where he was on a monthly basis. Without realizing the overall effect on the company, he took on additional product lines and became more aggressive in selling not only his services, but products. Six months into the fiscal year, the company's earnings were about $85,000, and he expected to reach $170,000 at year-end. In other words, things had changed. He was expanding. He required some of the profits to remain in the company to finance the growth. It was time to incorporate.

If he did not have monthly financial statements that triggered the incorporation, he would have had a personal liability for income taxes on $170,000 of earnings. The incorporation of the company in the seventh month eliminated $85,000 from his personal taxable income. This was taxed in the corporation at 25% or about $20,000 versus personal tax at 55% or $44,000. At that time, the corporation income tax for a small business was 25% on the first $200,000 of net profit. This was subsequently changed in the taxation year 1988 to 22% as part of the first stage of the Income Tax Reform.

Not only was the tax saving of $24,000 used to assist in the financing of the expanding company, but the corporate tax was not payable until some fifteen months after the company was incorporated.

Another example is a dehired middle manager who worked until June 30 and received $40,000 in pay with tax deductions on the basis of $80,000 of earnings for the year. It is quite common for a company to lose money in the first two to three or even up to six months of a start-up and then begin to break even, say in the seventh month. It may make sense for this individual to start his or her business as a proprietorship. If the proprietorship loses $40,000 before December 31 of that year and the owner makes the company year-end December 31, then the taxable income for the year will be $40,000 from the T4 less $40,000 from the business loss equals zero. This means that all of the tax deducted at source by the previous employer would be refunded by the government when the income tax return was filed.

Another thing to consider is the so-called prestige of incorporation. There are some who will suggest that anyone who starts a business and doesn't spend the $1,000 or so to incorporate really isn't in business. An unincorporated company may suffer more from the New Company Syndrome. You can see, then, that there is no simple answer to the question: "Do I incorporate?" It depends on your individual circumstances.

What Is Incorporation?

I would like to assume that in time your company requires that you incorporate to take advantage of tax planning. So, let's look at what an incorporated company really is. You first have to determine a name for the company and whether you want the name to be followed by Limited, Inc., Corporation, or whatever. The name must be cleared through a central registry and approved. In the case of our company, I really wanted the name to be Cunningham & Associates Inc.

However, we were unable to get approval because we were informed there were other Cunninghams. Therefore, the name of our company is G.G. Cunningham & Associates Inc. to differentiate which Cunningham. Sometimes choosing a name can be difficult from the outset, but then getting approval can be even more difficult. It is a good idea to have several names in mind in order that one will be available for your corporate name. If worst comes to worst, you can ask your lawyer for a numbered company. You can change the name at a later date when you are not so pressed for time.

Many of you will wish to follow the "lean and mean" and "stingy" approach in order to save money in your start-up. Well, when it's time to incorporate, I believe that you should pay the extra $300 to $500 at the outset to have the incorporation done properly by a lawyer. He or she will be able to get clearance of the name very quickly and assuming the lawyer is doing a good job, you will have no problems with expediting your start-up.

Share Structure

You must now determine the share structure for your incorporated company. Simple is best. There are many variations of the types of shares that can be included in your company, such as common shares, preferred shares, and convertible preferred shares, for example. In general, common shares are participating, meaning that they share in the growth of the company and are voting. However, there can be variations of this for tax-planning and estate-planning purposes. Class A common shares can mean voting and participating. Class B common shares can be participating and non-voting. Preferred shares are non-participating and generally non-voting except under special circumstances and usually have a dividend rate attached. For example, 7% cumulative or 7% noncumulative. The cumulative 7% dividends means that at the end of each year 7% of the cost of the preferred shares would be for distribution to the shareholder that year or at some time in the future. Noncumulative means that if the dividend is not declared in any year, it is not accumulated for the next year.

Convertible preferred shares are sometimes used when venture capital investment is in place. The venture capitalist is looking at a return on investment and the convertible privilege means that these shares can be converted on a formula basis to common shares. In fact, they participate in the increased value of the company.

Generally, only common shares are required. This is the simple approach.

One point to consider when structuring the share capital of your incorporated company is your spouse. If you are married, then let it be known that 50% of your new business will effectively be owned by your spouse through the various provincial Family Law Acts across Canada. You may wish to consider using the Class A common participating and voting and the Class B participating and non-voting shares for your structure. By issuing one Class A share to yourself and one Class B share to your spouse for one dollar, you can effectively split any possible future capital gains and dividends. (Your personal investment in the company should be in the form of a note payable or a shareholders' loan. This will allow you to recover your personal investment without any legal or tax implications.) For example, there is a $500,000 capital gains exemption on the sale of shares of Canadian-controlled private corporations (that's your small business). There are other details of qualification which will be discussed in Chapter 4. If you sell the shares for, say, $1,000,000, then you will effectively have sold the company for $1,000,000 tax free—$500,000 each. Like it or not, however, your spouse effectively owns 50% of the new venture. This can only be changed if you have your spouse sign a matrimonial contract which excludes the business from the matrimonial assets.

Officers and Directors

Once the company is formed, you must appoint officers and directors. If you wish, you can be the only officer and the only director. Some small-business owners wonder if they should form a board of directors to provide some advice and direction as the company proceeds through the start-up, development, and growth stages. It is fair to say that anyone familiar with the liability of directors would refuse to be a director, but happy to participate in an advisory panel which is discussed later on in Chapter 7.

As a director, you have potential liabilities in the event of failure of your company. The key items are employee deductions, sales tax, both federal and provincial, corporate income tax, and workers' compensation. You can also suffer personal third-party liability for negligence.

4

BUYING A BUSINESS OR FRANCHISE

One alternative to starting your business from scratch, which we discussed in Chapter 2, is to buy an on-going business in the sector of your choice. The good news is that you will be sidestepping the New Company Syndrome because the company purchased will have a track record and you will have made a substantial financial commitment when purchasing. Although Murphy's Law is still hiding in the shadows, it is not as prominent as in a start-up operation.

Buying a business with a proven track record of profits can almost guarantee its success and continuing operation. The chance of failure is much less than in a start-up. This assumes, of course, that you have not paid too much for the company and that you can service the debt incurred in order to finance the purchase. I generally recommend that individuals wishing to buy themselves a job, buy themselves a business instead of starting from scratch.

The main disadvantage of purchasing a business is that you will be paying for "goodwill." In simple terms, goodwill is the price you will pay for the business in excess of the actual assets that are purchased. There are two basic approaches to buying a business. First, the common approach is to purchase the operating assets (inventory, net fixed assets, and goodwill). The second approach is to purchase the shares from the owner. Traditionally, the vendor likes to sell shares and the purchaser likes to purchase assets.

The vendor likes to sell shares because—assuming the shares are held personally—the first $500,000 of selling price is tax free and only 75% of the amount over $500,000 is taxable. If the vendor sells assets (that includes goodwill), the company will be required to pay corporation tax on 75% of the goodwill. In addition, all of the cash resulting from the sale will be in the company's name. The vendor will be required to pay personal tax on some of the amounts to be distributed if the vendor company is to be wound up. Some vendors are very anxious to sell shares, get their money, and not be bothered with further details of the company. On the other hand, the purchaser wants to buy assets because 75% of the goodwill can be deducted for tax purposes over future years of the company's operation. The second major advantage to buying assets is that all of the debt is included in the company. This means that the net cash profit in the company can be used to pay down the debt. If you purchase shares, you will be required to form a holding company to buy the shares and then probably amalgamate the two companies at some future time in order to minimize the income-tax consequences.

You must also be cautious in buying a business as you might be paying for "ill will," caused by the inadequate service provided by the current owner.

There are four major problems with purchasing a business: 1. locating the right business; 2. valuing to determine price; 3. structuring the deal; 4. financing. It is fair to say that for every one business for sale, there are twenty people looking to buy. So, what is the best approach? There are advertisements in federal and provincial publications and national magazines that can be followed up. Another approach is to contact business brokers or consultants who specialize in the sale of businesses. In some cases, public accountants and bankers have information about potential vendors. The main problem with the above approaches is that many owners are concerned with confidentiality. They don't want employees, suppliers, or customers to know that they wish to sell. For this reason, they are reluctant to let business brokers, accountants, bankers, or anyone else know that they wish to retire or sell their business.

The best method, in my opinion, is the direct approach.

Once you have determined the type of business you want, then zero in on that area. In other words, seek out a business where the owner is approaching retirement years and make a direct approach on a confidential basis. Leads to potential vendors can be obtained by contacting the respective trade association in an effort to get a list of the members and possibly through discussion, obtain some information regarding the age of the respective owners. In some cases, this is better done through an intermediary, such as your accountant or a business consultant who can maintain the confidentiality both on behalf of the vendor and the purchaser. If you happen to be employed at the present time, you will not want your current employer to realize that you are planning to purchase another business and to leave his or her employ.

Valuation to Determine Price
Once you have located a possible vendor, then the next job is to get a handle on the value of the business. The income-tax implications and the structure of the deal are dealt with later on in the chapter. Virtually all purchases of small businesses are for operating assets which consist of inventory, net fixed assets, and goodwill. Valuing any business is a specialized area and the services of an accountant or business consultant skilled in mergers and acquisitions should be engaged to assist in valuing the business. However, it is possible for you to get a handle on the value for yourself before incurring the expense of professional services. For example, if you ascertain that the vendor wishes $500,000 for the operating assets and goodwill of his or her company, and your ballpark valuation is $300,000, then you probably have no basis upon which to continue further negotiations. If, however, your ballpark valuation is in the $400,000 to $450,000 area, then it would be appropriate to engage the services of a professional to help you finalize the purchase. Here is a good approach that you may use to make your own ballpark valuation.

Indicated Earnings
There are two major factors required to determine a reasonable value for any small business: *indicated earnings* and

earnings multiplier. The indicated earnings are the normal annual earnings before income tax that you can expect when you purchase the business. This means that you must adjust all expenses to reflect reasonable charges for wages of the owner, staff, and all operating expenses. To do this, request the last three years' financial statements from the vendor. The expenses should be reviewed with the vendor to eliminate any excess expenses that would not be included when you purchase the business, and add any additional expenses that may be incurred when you purchase the business. For example, the present owner may have taken $200,000 as his or her remuneration. If $75,000 is reasonable, then $125,000 should be added to the profit for the calculation of indicated earnings. Likewise, the owner may have taken his or her remuneration by dividends and no salary. So, in this example, $75,000 would have to be added to the expenses.

You will also be required to review the details of the vendor company's lease. Some key questions are: What is the term of the lease? What are the costs for the basic rent, acceleration clauses for increased expenses, percentage rent, and any common-area costs? Is the space adequate for reasonable expansion, or is there too much space and can some of this excess space be sublet? You must be aware of what is happening nearby: for example, is competition starting up, is the area slated for rezoning, and so forth.

The 1980s was the era of the wholesale/retail outlet. There are retailers that have been caught by a warehouse super-discount operation opening in the vicinity; consequently, it is important to determine what type of competition might be forthcoming in the near future before you sign on the dotted line.

Although buying a business eliminates the New Company Syndrome, Murphy is still lurking in the corner. An example is an individual who bought his job by buying a retail operation on the main street of a small town in Ontario. Two months after closing the deal, the local authorities tore up the street for the installation of a new sewer system. The sales dropped by more than 30%, the company was in a loss position, and only upfront, good financial planning enabled him to survive.

If the adjusted earnings before income taxes over the past three years indicate an increase from year to year, and there are prospects that the trend will continue, then the indicated earnings could very well be the latest annual earnings before income taxes as adjusted. Future prospects should be discussed with the vendor to provide you with some assurance that the upward trend will continue. (In formal valuations, the valuator would probably calculate the average weighted earnings in the past five years to arrive at this figure. However, sometimes historic information is less meaningful than current.)

Let's look at the current financial statement of a potential vendor with the adjustments and ultimate calculation of the indicated earnings. In Exhibit 5, the net pre-tax earnings "per financial statement" is $155,000. On reviewing the statement, wages at 31% of gross profit appear low and other expenses at 22% of gross profit appear high. Let us assume that your analysis of the details indicates that the owner took his remuneration in the form of dividends, and there is no amount there for him and his wife who is working actively in the business. If we assume that a reasonable wage for both of them is $60,000, then you would increase the wage cost from $125,000 to $185,000. This brings the wages up to 46% of gross profit which is reasonable. Let's also assume that an analysis of other expenses includes $15,000 of finance costs (which are not included in calculating indicated earnings) and other expenses that would be nonrecurring if you purchased the business. The other expenses are, therefore, reduced from $90,000 to $75,000 or 19% of gross profit which appears reasonable. The resulting indicated earnings are, therefore, $110,000, not $155,000.

Earnings Multiplier
The next step is to determine the earnings multiplier. This is the reciprocal of the return on investment (ROI). The two items used to determine the return on investment are present interest rates and the premium for the risk involved in owning a small business. Let's face it, if you can retrieve, say, 10% pre-tax without risk, what kind of return should you receive with the risk of owning a small business? An

EXHIBIT 5

CALCULATION OF INDICATED EARNINGS
($000s omitted)

	Per Financial Statement		Adjustments	Indicated Earnings	
Sales	$1,000		$—	$1,300	
Gross Profit	400	40%	$—	400	
		% of Gross Profit			% of Gross Profit
Expenses					
Wages	125	31	+60	185	46
Occupancy	30	8	—	30	8
Other	90	22	−15	75	19
Total	245	61	45	290	73
Net Pre-Tax Earnings	$ 155	39	−45	$ 110	27

accepted yardstick is 2.5 times the bank prime rate. This is an academic calculation and is normally adjusted upwards as a premium or reduced by discounting based on the state of the industry, the economic environment, the location, and other details regarding the specific industry. (This is where some outside assistance may be required.)

For example, if the indicated earnings have been increasing over the past few years at, say, 30% or 40% per year and the trend appears to be continuing, then the risk factor might be considered lower and you may be happy to accept a lower return on investment based on the indicated earnings. This increases the earnings multiplier. On the other hand, if the indicated earnings for the past three years have leveled off or have shown some decline, then you may consider this more risky than at the level suggested above and you may wish to value the business with a higher return on investment and, therefore, a lower earnings multiplier.

By reviewing the past prime interest rates, you will notice that there is quite a variation over the years. In fact, during 1989, the bank prime rate increased more than 35% from the year before. So, some may suggest that using the current prime rate may result in too high a return on investment and effectively too low a value for the business. But you must remember that you may be borrowing most, if not all, of the money to finance the project. You will be paying prime rate plus 2% or even 3%. Your return on investment must be adequate to pay for the interest and the principal and to provide financing for any expansion.

If the bank prime rate is 13.5%, then a reasonable return is, say, 33% (13.5% times 2.5), which converts to a 3 times multiplier (100 divided by 33%). In Exhibit 6, you will notice that the $110,000 of indicated earnings times the multiplier of 3 equals the value of the operating assets of a normal business, $330,000. However, let's assume that you have investigated the business, the location, the economic environment, and so forth and feel that this business is less risky and is worth more. You may wish to add a premium of say 20%. The earnings multiplier will then be increased to 3.6 (3.0 times 120%), providing a value of $396,000, say $400,000. The value varies, therefore, between $330,000 and $400,000.

EXHIBIT 6

NOTIONAL VALUE OF OPERATING ASSETS

Indicated Earnings	$110,000
Earnings Multiplier	3.0
Value of Normal Small Business . . .	$330,000
Premium	20%
High Value Multiplier	3.6
High Value	$396,000
Selling Price	$330,000 – $400,000

If the vendor is looking for $600,000, then you will know immediately that you will be unable to consummate a reasonable deal in the near future. However, if he or she had proper counseling, then the vendor may come back with another figure which would be in an area that could be negotiated.

Price vs. Value

The above calculations provide you with what is referred to as *notional value*. This is the value that could be used for estate planning and for situations where no one is looking to purchase or sell the business. You may consider this a yardstick. In many cases, price is quite different from value. Price is what a purchaser will pay and the vendor accept for the assets or shares of a business. You may be impatient and wish to get the show on the road and, although the top value may be $400,000, you may end up agreeing to pay $450,000 to $500,000 in order to "buy yourself a job."

If this is the case, instead of paying off your indebtedness in five to seven years, you are extending your repayment period to eight to ten years. On the other hand, you may review the operation of the business and observe some economies that you can implement that will increase the indicated earnings from $110,000 to, say, $150,000 and, therefore, you may be willing to pay $450,000 to $500,000. At this point, professional counseling is a necessity.

Structuring the Deal

The income tax implications on the purchase of a business are extremely important. In some cases, the structuring can make or break a deal. As mentioned earlier, there is an advantage to the vendor in selling shares; it has now been accentuated by the income tax system. The vendor is eligible for a capital gains exemption of up to $500,000 on the sale of shares of a small business. However, many business owners have substantial assets on the balance sheet. These can be excess cash, a condo in Florida, marketable securities, real estate, and so forth. These redundant assets must be removed from the balance sheet before selling the shares to any purchaser in order to conform with the "90% rule," which

EXHIBIT 7

CALCULATION OF GOODWILL

Inventory	$150,000
Fixed Assets (Net)	50,000
	200,000
Purchase Price	375,000
Goodwill	$175,000

Estimated Income Taxes

Taxable goodwill at 75%	$131,250	
Income tax at 22%		
(assume total taxable income		
for fiscal year under		
$200,000)		29,000
Net goodwill after income tax		$146,000

stipulates that 90% of the assets of a business must be used for the operation of the business in order to qualify for the capital gains exemption. In addition, to qualify, at least 50% of the operating assets of the vendor company must have been used in the operation of the business for two years prior to the sale. This can result in considerable income taxes for the vendor; it may offset any tax savings available through the $500,000 capital gains exemption. Consequently, in some cases, it may not be advantageous for the vendor to sell you shares.

Selling shares may appear to be a tax advantage to the vendor but it results in the elimination of the income tax write-off for goodwill that you, the buyer, could take advantage of (if you purchased the assets). For example, in Exhibit 7, we assume that the purchase price will be $375,000 for the operating assets and goodwill, so the resulting goodwill (after deducting inventory and the net fixed assets) is $175,000. But if you purchase shares, you will not be able to write off 75% of this goodwill, or about $130,000, against your taxable income over future years. Assuming your net profit from the business is under $200,000 a year, this represents about $29,000 of extra taxes that your company will have to pay at the small business tax rate of 22%.

In addition, the debt incurred to purchase shares can be more costly to you because it could be repaid with your after-tax personal dollars. A top marginal personal income tax rate is about 44%, and this means that the purchase price for the shares will be paid with after-tax dollars equivalent to fifty-six cents. If you were to purchase assets, the debt would remain in the company and be repaid out of after-tax corporate profits. The small business tax rate, assuming the profits to be under $200,000, is 22%. The debt can thus be paid with seventy-eight-cent dollars.

The cost of a share purchase can be minimized by forming a compay to purchase the shares which will incur the debt for the purchase and then amalgamating this company with the purchased company after closing the purchase. This will, in effect, transfer the debt from the holding company to the operating company and will be similar to that of purchasing assets. However, you will still not be able to write off any goodwill against income taxes and you will be required to spend a few thousand dollars to form the new company and amalgamate.

The only good news in buying shares is that the value of the shares is somewhat less than the value of the operating assets. The value of the shares is in effect the adjusted shareholders' equity of the vendor company after theoretically selling off the operating assets and paying the necessary income taxes on the goodwill. The goodwill of $175,000 is taxed at 22% of 75% of that amount or about $29,000. The increase in the shareholders' equity is, therefore, $146,000. So, a reasonable purchase price for the shares to account for the necessary tax ramifications is $296,000 versus the $375,000 for the operating assets. (See Exhibit 8.) In normal circumstances, you can expect the value of shares to be about 70% to 80% of the value of the operating assets.

The message is clear. It is extremely important that you engage the services of an accounting firm that is experienced in mergers, acquisitions, and the income tax implications on the purchase of a business.

EXHIBIT 8

BALANCE SHEET
BEFORE SALE OF ASSETS AND GOODWILL
($000s omitted)

Assets		Liabilities	
Bank	$ 10	Accounts payable	$100
Accounts receivable	40		
Inventory	150		
Net fixed assets	50	Shareholders' equity	150
Total	$250	Total	$250

BALANCE SHEET
AFTER SALE OF ASSETS AND GOODWILL
($000s omitted)

Assets		Shareholders' Equity	
Bank	$296	Before sale	$150
		Add: Net goodwill	146
Total	$296	Total	$296

Buying a Franchise

Buying a franchise is a good news/bad news situation. The good news is that it is an easy way to buy yourself a job. The bad news is you really aren't your own boss, and in some cases the upfront franchise fee and the ongoing percentage royalty or franchise fee can be excessive.

However, buying a franchise is a viable option. There are literally hundreds of products and services that are available through franchised operations. Franchise shows are established at least annually where the franchisers can demonstrate the merits of their particular franchise. For someone considering getting into his or her own business, these shows can provide not only leads to franchise operations, but that "idea" you need if you want to start up your own business or buy an existing business.

Let's look at the wonderful world of franchising. When you take on a franchise, you obtain the right to use the franchiser's name and public image. You will find that financing is more readily available. Your upfront financial commitment can be less than if you were buying a business. As a franchisee, you get the benefits of belonging to a large organization, while remaining, to some degree, your own boss. Your business gets the name recognition and consumer confidence of the large firm. Studies prove that franchises have a lower failure rate than other independently owned firms. That's because of the tried and true advertising, training programs, and systems and procedures established by the franchiser. You should know too that franchising is one of the fastest growing business trends in North America. *Tomorrow's customer*, a publication of Ernst and Young, indicates that the trends in franchising as a percentage of total retail sales was 36% in 1985 and forecasted to increase to 50% in 1990 and 55% in 1995.

But don't let that lull you into a sense of complacency. There are examples of failures. Some franchisees fail, but it is not apparent because there is no visible change to the public. The franchiser, in other words, has obtained a new franchisee to take the position of the failed small-business owner. Although a franchiser can, in many cases, provide planning, training, promotional assistance, and advice, the onus is still on you to make your franchise succeed.

Many aspiring new business owners are very high on enthusiasm but very low in expertise. Franchising can provide much of the upfront work involved in a start-up. In most cases, the franchiser provides a site, negotiates the lease and, in some cases, may provide a turn-key operation. "A turn-key operation" means just that. After you have paid your franchise fee, taken your training course, and signed the contract, the franchiser literally hands you a key to a business that is fully operational from the outset. Many of the normal start-up problems are handled by the experts. Many suppliers will give you reasonable payment terms. Although the franchiser will not guarantee your bank loan, there is a feeling of comfort with some bankers on reviewing your business plan for the financing proposal.

When you take on a franchise, you have, in fact, somewhat compromised your position of independence. You will be required to manage the operation by "the book." (For many, that's a blessing in disguise.) You are really a cross between a manager and an owner.

One problem is the financial arrangements. Once you have paid the upfront franchise fee and financed the equipment and renovations necessary for the franchise operation, you will find yourself paying a percentage franchise fee forever. In addition to the franchise fee, you can expect to pay an advertising fee. Usually such fees are calculated as a percentage of sales. The fees can range anywhere from 5% to 15%, depending on the business. However, there are some franchises that make their profit by selling products that are marked up to account for the franchiser's remuneration.

Another problem comes up when it is time to sell. Many franchise agreements place some restrictions on the sale. You can find yourself only receiving book value for your many years of hard work. In other words, no goodwill is associated with the sale, and you end up getting paid only for your inventory and your net fixed assets. If the franchise is earning $100,000 a year, then it is possible that you are automatically waiving any right to, say, $200,000 to $300,000 of goodwill on sale.

Buying a franchise is an easy way to get started to build up personal equity. It is better than working for a straight salary, but you will not attain the equity that you might if you had bought a business or had a successful start-up.

So, how do you locate a suitable franchise? Review the various franchises available. It is a good idea to contact the Association of Canadian Franchisers to obtain any details on the various franchises that are available in Canada. Once you have decided on the industry, then obtain details of at least two franchises in the industry that you might be considering.

Here's where another problem begins. The literature supplied by many franchise operations is four-color glossy and has financial data that sometimes suggests that the franchise is a gold mine. You can be sure of one thing: the financial forecasts included are very enthusiastic.

The next step is to meet with officials of the two franchises and plan a visit to at least two operating franchises for each company. Determine how many franchisees are operating successfully. Remember, if your operation doesn't make a profit after the franchise fee, you are virtually back to working for salary with the added headache of operating as though you were in your own business.

When visiting franchisees, confirm with the owners their start-up costs, operating costs, and actual sales. Equally important, find out whether the franchiser has fulfilled its commitment for management backup. One way to gauge the franchiser's sincerity and assistance to make you a successful franchisee is the scope of its operations' manual. There should be a simple bookkeeping system to provide you with basic information on a daily, weekly, and monthly basis. If not, regard this franchise with suspicion. A comprehensive operations' manual is the mark of a truly reputable franchiser.

It also is important for anyone interested in taking on a franchise to recognize that many of the legal battles between franchiser and franchisee are caused by the latter's lack of understanding of the franchise agreement. Therefore, it is advisable to seek assistance from a competent lawyer before signing the agreement. Lawyers specializing in franchises are recommended.

There are three general types of franchisers: those who are reputable, those who are con men, and those who are fraudulent.

There are many reputable franchisers who provide legitimate proven systems that allow an individual to buy himself or herself a job and to earn a reasonable profit. However, con franchises also exist that have been developed with very little support and a limited operations' manual. These owners are required to sell franchises as quickly as possible in order to obtain the up-front franchise fee to finance their business.

Most of these franchisers offer four-color glossy brochures with extremely optimistic profit forecasts. The worst kind, of course, are the fraudulent franchisers who misrepresent their franchise and deceive people into thinking they will be millionaires. The 1980s saw details of some of these on the front pages of Canadian newspapers. I hope that the above information will allow you to qualify any franchiser you may be dealing with. Under no circumstances should you deal with any but the reputable.

5

FEASIBILITY

You now have an idea for your product or service and you know in which sector of the marketing chain you'll be involved. The next step is crucial because you will start spending possibly a great deal of your hard-earned money. You must decide whether your idea will successfully translate into a worthwhile commercial venture or whether it is just one of the great ideas that may never get off the ground.

The time has come to perform some research to determine the viability and feasibility of your idea. This means that you must gather pertinent information on both the marketing of the idea and the costs associated with getting your product or service into the marketplace.

Although we will deal primarily with a start-up situation, the same research also applies to determine the viability of any company or franchise you may wish to purchase.

Once again, we shall address these issues as they relate to the five sectors: manufacturing, manufacturers' rep, wholesale, retail, and service.

Break-even Calculation
Determining the feasibility of any business eventually comes down to a simple calculation which is called the "break-even point." In other words, what sales are required to cover the direct costs associated with the realization of your idea. Here is the formula:

$$\frac{\text{Total operating expenses}}{\text{Gross profit percentage}} = \text{Break-even sales}$$

For example, if the operating expenses for the year for wages, occupancy, and so forth are estimated at $150,000 and the gross profit percentage is thirty, then the break-even point is:

$$\frac{\$150,000}{30\%} = \$500,000*$$

To calculate the break-even point for the venture, you must determine the estimated operating expenses and the gross profit percentage. To calculate the gross profit percentage of a single product, you must determine the selling price and the material costs. For example, if the selling price is projected at $10 and the material cost in the product is $7, then the gross profit is $3. This means the gross profit is 30%. If you will be marketing several products, then the gross profit percentage should be calculated for each of the products and the sales mix of the individual products must be determined in order to arrive at an aggregate average gross profit percentage. For example, if you estimate sales of, say, $50,000 each for five different products and the gross profit percentages for the various items are 20%, 25%, 30%, 35%, and 40%, respectively, then the gross profit estimated for the total operation would be the average of these gross profits. In other words, 20% of $50,000 added to 25% of the $50,000 for the next product and so forth means a gross profit total of $75,000. The sales projected are $250,000. This means that the gross profit for the total operation is 30% ($75,000 divided by $250,000 times 100). This applies to the manufacturing, wholesaling, and retailing operations where the gross profit of the individual products may be different but, in some cases, the overall is reasonably predictable.

$$*\frac{\$150,000 \times 100}{30} = \$500,000$$

Gross Profit %	Estimated Sales $50,000 for 5 Products				
	A	B	C	D	E
20%	$10,000				
25%		$12,500			
30%			$15,000		
35%				$17,500	
40%					$20,000
Total					$75,000

Total Estimated Sales	$250,000
Gross Profit	$75,000
Gross Profit as a % of sales	30%

As we suggested in Chapter 2, these percentages vary within sectors depending on the industry. The break-even point of most service-sector companies will be the total of the operating costs. However, in the case of dry cleaning stores, there is usually an 8% to 10% variable cost for materials or supplies in cleaning the garments. Therefore, in this case, the formula would include the gross profit percentage of 90% to 92%.

To determine the selling price of your product you must examine the competition. The big guys conduct costly detailed market-research studies to arrive at selling prices before they put any new products on the market. To their minds, spending money upfront to be certain that a product is viable in the marketplace is worthwhile. You needn't be intimidated by market research, however, because you can conduct what I call a market analysis, thereby acquiring an overview and arriving at similar conclusions.

In other words, whether you have a product or service, seek out the competition, determine their pricing, and how they are operating. In addition, you should be in personal contact with potential customers. For your own business, you can conduct market interviews on your own. The target market will be the type of people who are potential purchasers of the product or your service. If it is a high-quality expensive consumer product or service, then there is no point having interviews with individuals who cannot afford to purchase it or will never need this service. Likewise, if it is an inexpensive item that the wealthy would not be interested in purchasing, then you should really be dealing with the person on the street to get his or her input. You can talk to your good friends and family, but you must monitor the sincerity of their response. You don't want to be patted on the back and told you have a great idea. What you want are hard, real comments about the product or service.

You may wish to engage the services of a consultant to assist you in developing the appropriate market-analysis program. He or she can also help develop a questionnaire to interview target markets. One inexpensive approach is to use the consulting services established for this purpose in business schools across Canada. The students from these services will also conduct the interviews at a reasonable cost.

In conducting any interviews, it is important to be sure that you are getting the right answers from the people interviewed, not the ones you want to hear. It has been suggested that on receipt of a positive response, you should ask the interviewee if he or she would like to invest money in your business. If you receive a quick no, then you have to determine the credibility of the previous answers.

Once you have completed approximately 60 interviews and you feel comfortable that the comments are truthful, it is time to analyze the details. You now know something about your competition and potential customers. Based on this, you must determine what a reasonable selling price would be for your products or services. Additional details are set out in Chapter 11.

The next step is to determine the material costs. For a wholesaler and retailer, the costs are obvious. However, a manufacturer needs to spend more time determining these. Details of the manufacturing sector are set out later in the chapter.

Finally, you must determine the operating costs for the new business. This means determining the wages for you and your staff and the other expenses for the marketing, operations, and administration of your new business. Details of operating costs by sector are dealt with later in the chapter.

If your operating costs amount to $10,000 per month, for example, and your gross profit is 25%, then your break-even point is $40,000 per month ($10,000 times 100 over 25). The next question: "Is it feasible to sell $40,000 per month?" Granted, this may not be done in the initial months. But you should expect adequate sales to break even within the first six months. If this seems reasonable, then all stations are go. If not, it's back to the drawing board to revise your plan or possibly stop here before you spend any more of your hard-earned money.

Going back to the drawing board means analyzing the expenses that amount to $10,000 per month with a view to reducing. And to review the gross profit percentage with a view to increasing. This can be done by increasing the selling price or decreasing the material costs through better purchasing. Determining the break-even point or the feasibility of your project is purely a mathematical calculation. Varying the components of the total operating expenses and the gross profit percentage has a direct effect on the ultimate break-even point. For example, if the expenses of $10,000 per month can be reduced to $8,000 while maintaining the same gross profit percentage, then the break-even point is $32,000 ($8,000 times 100 over 25) or a reduction of $8,000 in sales per month. Likewise, if you can increase the gross profit percentage from 25% to 30% while maintaining the $10,000 of operating expenses, then the break-even point is $33,333 ($10,000 times 100 over 30).

In both cases, the reduction in the break-even point is about 20%. This can mean the difference between starting and not starting your business.

Conversely, an increase in the operating expenses from $10,000 to $12,000 will increase the break-even point to $48,000. A decrease in the gross profit percentage from 25% to 20% will increase the break-even point to $50,000 ($10,000 divided by 100 over 20). The key to a successful start-up, therefore, is to maintain a stingy approach to incurring any ongoing expenses for wages, rent, supplies, and any other expenses. In addition, pricing a product (this will be discussed in Chapter 11) sometimes becomes the ultimate decision-maker for any successful start-up.

This is where some of the big-company downsized executives have a problem. It is really an attitude problem. For the past 15 to 20 years, they worked in big-company environments where there were ample, if not excessive, support services for their activities. At the time, they wouldn't have agreed, but a person with a sharp pencil and a keen eye for productivity might suggest that these executives were pampered. This can be the major mental barrier to hurdle. When you are in your own business, you must take your jacket off, roll up your sleeves, and be prepared to perform any of the tasks necessary. I remember hearing an executive who left a big company and started his own business laugh at having to wash the windows from time to time. The good news is that his business has grown, and now this is being handled by support staff. In this case, he was able to make the necessary change in attitude for the start-up to succeed.

As you progress through this initial thinking, you will find that you will make all of the decisions yourself. This is a far cry from the committee approach to decision-making that you have been used to. At this point, it is a good idea to contact your accountant, consultant, or other business advisors who can review the various alternative break-even analyses. This will give you an outside objective opinion on the feasibility of your new venture. (Engaging the services of an accountant, consultant, and establishing an advisory panel will be dealt with in Chapter 7.)

If it's a go, then you have reached a major crossroad on the way to buying yourself a job and being your own boss. The next step is to develop your business plan which will be discussed in Chapter 6. A major part of the business plan will be a brief description of this feasibility study, the manner in which you intend to market your product, and the estimated cash requirements to finance the start-up adequately.

Marketing Chain

Let's take a look at the marketing chain. It is fair to say at this time that a manufacturer can obtain the highest numbers of unit sales by using the master-marketing chain: broker, wholesaler, retailer. Brokers can be engaged across Canada on a commission basis. They will have established wholesalers who in turn will have established retailers to sell to the end user. So the marketing network is established in very quick order. However, there is a cost.

Because each industry is different, I will set out some assumed gross profit percentages required by the individual sectors in the marketing chain. Let's assume that your product costs $10 and with a 30% gross profit, your price to the broker is $14.30. (This is calculated by dividing the $10 by the reciprocal of the gross profit percentage: $10 divided by 100 over 70). Although the broker does not take possession, he or she will want 10% so that the selling price to the wholesaler will be $15.90 ($14.30 divided by 100 over 90). The wholesaler will then sell it to the retailer at a 30% gross profit for $22.70 ($15.90 divided by 100 over 70). The retailer will ultimately sell it at full list at 40% for $37.80 ($22.70 divided by 100 over 60). The message is clear. Regardless of your place in the marketing chain, you must determine what price a product should sell for in order for you to obtain the optimum return. The higher the price, the higher the gross profit, and no doubt the lower the unit sales. And the lower the price, the lower the gross profit, and no doubt the higher the unit sales.

A Feasibility Study: Manufacturing Sector

Let's look at a manufacturing start-up where you have developed a product that you can manufacture and sell in a niche market, either locally or nationally. You must have a prototype made for demonstration purposes. This will give you a handle on the time involved to manufacture the product and the cost of the specific materials required.

It is possible that you can make this prototype yourself in your basement or utilize the services of some of the incubation centers set up across Canada. Another approach is to contact a small manufacturing company that might make the prototype for you. In this case, you should get an upfront confirmed price on the cost and have a confidentiality agreement signed by the manufacturer. This will provide some protection from the manufacturer stealing your great idea. If you are convinced that this is the idea of the decade, then you may wish to take steps to have the item patented. Initiation of the patent process will give you the necessary protection. Nonetheless, it is still a good idea to have a confidentiality form signed by the manufacturer.

Let's assume that your analysis of the market suggests that a reasonable selling price at the retail level is $40. The next step is to review the competition. Although your product may be unique, it will be satisfying a consumer need that no doubt could also be satisfied by products of a similar nature. If these products are in the $20-bracket, then you must determine the advantages of your product to offset the price differential. If competition is in the $60-bracket, then you must review their product to see what advantages it has over yours. In any event, you must determine where you stand by this price and quality comparison.

The next step is to determine the cost of the product. This can be done by personal analysis or by consulting the manufacturing firm that made the prototype. The manufacturer should provide prices on sliding scales for various quantities; for example, 1,000, 10,000, 20,000, and so forth. The unit costs will, no doubt, be lower with the higher volume purchasing.

Based on your analysis, you should determine what a reasonable purchase run should be after you have launched the product. The cost at this level should be the cost used in determining your gross profit percentage. The next step is to have a minimum number of items manufactured (at a higher cost) and do some detailed testing, like the big guys, in some of the local stores. At this point, you will act as the wholesaler as well as the manufacturer in order to test the viability of the project further. In two or three months, you will have feedback from the store owners as to the acceptability of the product and, of course, the price.

If you determine that a realistic selling price is $40, and the manufacturer will sell you the product in reasonable quantities for, say, $10, then you are able to determine your marketing plan for your new product.

Based on the market analysis, a selling price of $40 will enable you to market your product through the master-marketing chain. However, if the market analysis indicates that a reasonable selling price is $30, then you would have to review the marketing chain and come up with an alternative plan. This means eliminating some of the intermediaries or negotiating a lower gross profit for the group or negotiating a better cost from your subcontracting manufacturer. By the way, an $8 cost would allow you to utilize the suggested master-marketing chain and sell the product at retail for $30.27. However, if this is not feasible or if you are required to commit yourself to excessive runs—20,000 versus 10,000, for example—then the alternative is to look to the present marketing chain and negotiate lower gross profits.

If you have a new dynamic product that will be a fast mover, the wholesalers and retailers may accept a lower gross profit percentage in order to have the product priced properly for quick turnover. In addition, your own pricing strategy may be to have a lower gross profit and a higher volume. Therefore, if you reduce your gross profit from 30% to 25%, reduce the wholesaler from 30% to 25%, the retailer from 40% to 35%, and cut out the broker, the list price for the $10-cost product can be $27.28.

Based on this analysis, you will be able to determine a method of marketing any new product. There are examples of start-ups where the reasonable selling price to the consumer did not allow for middle men. An example is Alex Tilley who spearheaded the start-up of his business by selling his product directly to the end user. He did this through his own stores and his national mail-order system. However, with higher volume and lower costs, he was able to establish some outside retailer operations in North America. It is fair to say that to get the best results and the highest number of sales, you must give the middle men or your marketing chain, a reasonable percentage. These people are the key to your success, and they must make a reasonable return for their efforts.

Retail Sector

You have now determined which industry you will be involved in and what products or product lines you will be selling. Next determine "What business am I really in."

Three Types of Retailers: Which One Are You?
There are three basic types of retailers: super discount, normal, and full service. Super discount is exactly that. They have over 15,000 plus square feet, sell products well below the manufacturers' normal list price, and provide minimal personal service. The full-service retailer will do very little discounting and develop a quality image for the upscale market. The normal store will be a cross section between the above two and will have some discounted sales from time to time as part of its marketing strategy to increase activity.

You cannot be all things to all people. You must determine the trend that you wish to follow. You cannot have a super-discount store with 1,000 square feet. Likewise, it is difficult to give full custom service in 20,000 square feet. The pricing strategy for your products must be governed by the business you are "really in." Once you have determined this, you will be able to estimate your gross profit percentage. Obviously, the full-service retailer will have the highest percentage and this could be in the area of 40% to 45%. A normal retailer will probably drop to between 30% to 35% and the super-discount store will be in the 20% to 25% bracket.

Location
The next step is to find a location for your new retail operation. The location of your business will also be decided by the business that you are "really in." There is no point in having a super-discount operation in a prestigious residential area. Likewise, there is no point in having a full-service operation with high-quality, high-priced products in a low-rental district.

You must determine your target market and locate accordingly. Residents in different regional areas within the city, let alone the country, have different requirements and different needs. The requirements in the various ethnic communities may be different as well.

Consequently, you must conduct some initial research before finalizing any lease arrangements for your new store. This demographic information may be available at the local boards of trade, chambers of commerce, and from commercial companies such as CompuSearch Market and Social Research Limited.

Location and Leasing

The location and lease you enter into can make or break your company. I have seen many examples of retailers starting up in malls with too much space and a bad lease. The high cost per foot, compounded by a percentage of sales, can eliminate any hope of profits for some of these retailers. A retail start-up is difficult at the best of times, but when 30% to 50% of the gross profit is being dedicated to the landlord, then you can expect losses in the first five years. Obviously, many cannot last that long, and they pack it in. All too often, retail start-ups get caught in the Traffic Syndrome. The Traffic Syndrome occurs when retailers pay for great numbers of people to walk by their door. Small-business owners get caught up in these heavy costs when the traffic doesn't warrant such costs. Many of the shopping malls in Canada are providing incentive leases for big companies who are referred to as anchor tenants, at the cost of excessive rents to small-business owners.

Over the years, I have developed an "eyeball" financial analysis for small-business owners who want to see where they stand. It is very simple. As a percentage of gross profit, wages and benefits should be no more than 50%, occupancy (rent, common area costs, utilities) 10%, and all other expenses 20%. This means that a target profit is 20% of the gross profit. This will vary from industry to industry, but is a general yardstick I use when industry statistics are not available (which is the case for most industries, by the way).

A few years ago, in one of my monthly columns in a national retail magazine, I set out the above formula. Letters to the editor were forthcoming from retailers from across Canada. The good news was that they were reading my column. The bad news was that they could not believe my factor of 10% for occupancy costs. Let me quote from one of the letters: "If you add the rent, light, heat and power, common expenses and taxes, you would be lucky to come out at 30% of gross profit. Could you please inquire from the author if there was, in fact, a misprint. . . ."

It is fair to say that small-business retailers are being gouged by the owners of shopping malls. With percentage rents of up to seven percent of gross sales, retailers can consider themselves in partnership with mall owners. This is confirmed by one headline in a Toronto newspaper: "Rising mall costs maul the little guy." Not only are the rents high, they are unpredictable. For example, some small-business retailers are sustaining increases that double their rents after five-year leases. According to one official at the Canadian Federation of Independent Business: "The uncertainty makes it impossible for retailers to budget." So much for the Traffic Syndrome.

There are alternatives that should be explored before you get caught up in the number of potential customers that you may have because of the high-priced location. Street fronts are becoming trendy and profitable for small-business owners, and the dominance of shopping centers is being challenged. The street-front shops have two advantages. One: they are less costly and, in my view, will produce more profit. Two: you are not tied to the hard-and-fast rules to which most malls subject all of their tenants. When you are in a mall, you have lost control of many decisions.

Having said all this, there is an example of a small chain of retail stores that operates in high-priced malls with a rent of 7% of sales and an occupancy cost running about 27% of the gross profit. In discussions with the owner, I was informed that he was not unhappy with the high rent because he could offset it by tighter management of the other expenses: wages (34% of gross profit) and other expenses (19% of gross profit). This retail owner has achieved the target profit of 20% of gross profit by operating a lean machine. He made a conscious effort as part of his planning process to obtain the highest possible gross profit for the individual products and to minimize the labor costs. Therefore, if you are excited about signing in a high-traffic, high-cost shopping mall, then you had better be prepared to be stingy and operate a lean machine.

Another problem for retailers other than percentage rent and location is the size of the store. In my view, the smaller the store, the better. There are two reasons for this. First, the rent is lower. And second, you don't have space to pile the inventory that you don't need. A small display area means that you can only afford to carry the winners. We will be talking about inventory control in Chapters 9 and 10. But you should bear in mind that 80% of sales comes from 20% of products. Know which products comprise the 20%—the winners—and you will not need most of the other items. The ideal is getting 50% of your sales from 50% of your products.

Location Analysis: What to Consider

There are other items that need to be investigated before any retailer signs on the dotted line:

1. Is the store readily accessible to the public?
2. Is there a reasonable traffic count to support your operation?
3. Are you congenial with the other stores? In other words, there is no point in putting a butcher shop in the middle of a high-fashion area.
4. Is there competition in the vicinity? In some cases, competition is good, especially if you are selling a high-priced product that customers wish to compare before buying. On the other hand, if you are selling a low-priced general product, then no other store of your type should be in this vicinity.
5. If you are locating in a small town, or in a suburban area, you should determine whether the population trends are upward or downward. In urban areas, population trends are unlikely to be dramatic, but there could be demographic swings that will affect your business.
6. What is the occupancy cost? (This includes the rent, utilities, common area costs, any acceleration due to increase in property taxes, and so forth.) Most percentage-rent leases will state the greater of the percentage of sales or the base rent. You should determine whether the total occupancy cost will turn your feasible new venture into a statistic: one of the 80% of small businesses that fail.
7. Find out if there are major construction plans for the area. For example, from time to time, major construction is undertaken to fix sewer drains, paving, and so

on. The disruption this would cause to business during the first year could be the death knell.

8. Check the zoning bylaws as each community will have municipal laws governing the operation of various types of businesses in various areas of a town or city. Recently, an individual spent his life savings setting up a restaurant bar in an area that was dry.

9. Assemble a profile on the local population to be certain that your product line is in demand in the area.

10. Determine if competition might be moving into your trading area in the near future.

Decisions on the location of manufacturing, wholesale, and service operations are based on different criteria than those listed above. However, municipal-zoning bylaws should be considered in decisions on location for businesses in any sector.

Negotiating the Lease

Once you have located what you feel are reasonable premises for your operation, then the next step is to approach the landlord and express your interest in leasing. The odds are you will be dealing with a property manager or real-estate agent acting on behalf of the landlord or owner. They will be pleased to complete the standard offer to lease form for presentation to the landlord. Under no circumstances should you sign this document at this time. I realize that the landlord will probably not wish to make any changes. However, you will be making a possibly fatal mistake if you do not march directly to your lawyer to get his or her blessing.

Paying a lawyer a fee to review an offer to lease that you probably can't change may seem like a waste of money. It's not. If you have engaged the services of a business lawyer, he or she will ask you some very straight questions about the business, the lease, the cost, some of the details in the offer to lease, and will fight for necessary changes. After discussions with your lawyer, if you and he or she agree that the terms are reasonable and within your budget, then by all means sign.

If you are incorporating your business from the outset,

then make sure that you sign the lease as president of the company and that the lease is in the company's name. If you sign it personally, then in the event of failure, you will be personally responsible for the rent and all additional costs until such time as the premises are leased to another party. However, I should point out that when the lease is finalized, you will no doubt be asked to sign personally and be personally responsible. It is possible, however, through proper negotiation to persuade the landlord that your personal guarantee is not necessary. (Don't hold your breath.)

Another common question is: "Should I buy or lease my premises?" There are two responding questions:

1. Do you have the money?
2. Do you want to be a landlord?

In virtually every start-up situation, the resounding answer to both questions is no. Although many have been caught up in real-estate fever in various parts of Canada in the late 1980s, you still have to ask yourself another question: "What business am I really in?" If it is the real-estate business, then you should perhaps buy your premises. If you are selling or making widgets, then perhaps you should leave the real-estate business to the people with the money and the skills in that area.

As a general rule, you can expect to pay on a net net lease anywhere from 8% to 12% of the value of the property you are leasing. By the way, net net means that the lease cost is for the basic facility, not including renovations, repairs and maintenance, property taxes, business taxes, utilities, or any other expenses related to the facility. The only exception might be major reconstruction, and this should be covered in the lease. Therefore, if we assume that a reasonable average is 10%, it means that if you are leasing a facility for $50,000, the market value is about $500,000. To purchase this property would mean a minimum of $100,000 down. At 12%, the mortgage interest alone is $48,000 a year. If you do not have $100,000 to put down, you may find yourself paying $15,000 interest on the down payment. In addition, you would be required to make some principal payments. Therefore, $50,000 rent could easily turn out to be a $75,000 expenditure on a purchase. If you expect the property to double in five years, then this may be a good investment. However, if you do not have the financing available for the purchase, then you may destroy your new venture before it gets off the ground in an effort to get greedy and look for long-term profit. Remember, you must be in business for the short term in order to be around for the long term.

After you have successfully been in business for several years, you may wish to consider another new business, which is real estate. If it is your own facility, then you can be guaranteed of a pretty good tenant. But the message is clear: Don't mix the two businesses in your new venture. Consider the purchase of a building as a second new business.

Another critical consideration is the amount of space you'll require to display and sell your line of products adequately. If you are considering confectionery items, then possibly a kiosk in some of the indoor shopping malls is appropriate. If it is stereo equipment, then you may require 1,000 square feet plus in order to display and market the products adequately. Each industry will have different space requirements. It is important, therefore, to analyze your own situation.

One of the major mistakes made by retailers who are starting up is to lease excessive space. The second mistake is to sign a bad lease with a high cost per square foot, and worst of all, a lease based on a percentage of sales. This really means you have taken on a partner before you have started.

At this point, you should summarize the details of the various expenses for operating your retail store. One of the key decisions you make at this time is the store hours. The longer the store is open, the higher the costs. If you are in a mall, then you will probably have no choice about the store hours. However, if you happen to be a stand-alone street-front operation where you have full control, then you should determine what days the store should be open, the hours (9:00 AM to 6:00 PM, 9:00 AM to 9:00 PM, and so forth). Once you are in business, of course, it is easy to monitor your sales. For example, if you are open from 9:00 AM to 9:00 PM and the activity between 7:00 PM and 9:00 PM is low, then you may wish to close the store at 7:00 PM.

Once this is decided, you should make a detailed list of the staff requirements for cashiers and full-time and part-time sales clerks. You also require a salary for yourself. Your second major cost will be for occupancy, and this will be governed by the lease you have signed and the other costs for common area, utilities, property taxes, and repairs and maintenance. Other expenses will include items such as advertising, credit card fees, delivery (if any), interest and bank charges, insurance, licences and fees, professional fees, store expenses, telephone, and possibly wrapping supplies. The respective trade association should be able to provide you with a list of the various types of expenses and possibly some statistics on the actual amounts by category. If this is not available, then you should review the details with your advisors.

Once you have determined your operating expenses and your gross profit percentage, you can calculate the break-even point. Remember, think lean and plan for as high a gross profit as possible. This will minimize your break-even point. If your calculation indicates that the sales required to break even are $50,000 per month, then you must determine if this is feasible. The factors to consider are many, and they're variable. Once you've reviewed them to the best of your ability, you should consult with your advisors, seeking as objective and critical an assessment from them as you can.

Wholesale Sector
Determining the feasibility of your wholesale operation is similar to determining feasibility in the retail sector.

Although the location is not as crucial to the wholesaler as it is to a retailer, it is still one of the most important decisions to make when starting up. One of your major costs will be delivery. Obviously, the closer you are to your customers, the lower the delivery cost. As in the retail operation, you must determine your target market. You must also decide the regional area you wish to deal with. It can be very difficult to have one warehouse and attempt to service Canada.

The odds are, your manufacturing suppliers will not be pleased with this, and it will not be cost effective for you. They may insist on more regional warehouses across Canada to provide sufficient warehousing services to their customers. You cannot be everything to everyone; instead, determine the regional area you wish to service and lease premises that are convenient and will allow you to provide the best service to your customers. The break-even sales should be calculated in the same manner as a retail operation.

Service Sector

Determining whether this new service start-up is feasible is much simpler than in the other sectors. In most cases, there is no gross profit for material costs. It is usually a case of adding up the various expenses and determining whether you can charge those amounts as fees. For example, if you were starting a consulting firm out of your home, the operating costs would be minimal: some advertising, auto, entertainment, and salary for yourself. If this amounts to $5,000 per month, then your break-even point is $5,000 per month. If you happen to be starting a dry cleaning operation, then the expenses would be higher as you would have occupancy costs as well as a material cost of, say, 8% to 10% for chemicals, hangers, and other supplies.

The location for the service-sector start-up is not as important as in the retail or wholesale sectors. Many make the mistake of opening an office in the downtown core because "That's where the action is." In fact, most of the business conducted by service industries, such as consulting firms, insurance agents, and so forth is in the client's office. In the case of our company, the first location after leaving the house was in the same building as our key client. This enabled us to provide better service, and it was also convenient to my home. Four moves later, we are within three miles of the original office and conveniently located for our out-of-town clients at the junction of Highways 404 and 401 in Metropolitan Toronto (with lots of free parking). Any suggestion that we should locate downtown has been eliminated.

As indicated before, 80% of start-up companies discontinue or fail within three to five years. Although no statistics are available, I would like to suggest that the majority of the 80% were not viable from the outset. I would further suggest that these individuals did not do their homework and did not determine the feasibility of their projects. I suspect that they did not prepare a proper business plan, which includes a marketing plan, before they started paying out some big bucks to buy their job.

They say that experience is a great teacher. Well, I was involved with launching a new educational product in the late 1960s. It was a new concept and a major purchase for the public-school system and commercial-training organizations. We followed the steps set out above: had a great idea; talked to respective people in the industry; made a prototype; tested the prototype in a schoolroom; and gave demonstrations to senior educational officials from OISE (Ontario Institute of Studies in Education). The result: One is in every classroom. The next step was to have ten manufactured for sale and demonstration purposes and more research.

Our marketing plan was to establish dealers selling directly to the educational systems and large commercial organizations with strong training programs. We knew our costs and established a reasonable selling price. This allowed a gross profit of about 40% for the dealer and about 30% for us. The operating costs were minimal. They included my salary and a secretary's, travel expenses, some advertising, and the occupancy cost. The break-even point was reasonable, and our enthusiasm and confidence was at an all-time high.

We participated in government-sponsored trade missions to New York, Chicago, and London, England. Dealerships were set up in England, in the United States, and in British Columbia, Alberta, and Ontario. Comments from enthusiastic supporters included: "Please let us know when you go public."

Some of the strong supporters insisted that the worst thing that could happen was to be unable to provide for the demand. This resulted in ordering 50 units at $2,000 per unit (1968 dollars). When the dust settled two years later, the only sales to the educational systems were made by us. None of the dealers was able to sell the units. We changed the marketing approach in order to sell direct to the end users, but this required additional financing. In the end, the company was sold to a venture capitalist who continued with the operation.

The lesson to be learned is that you cannot necessarily rely on comments from the experts who have no money on the line for the project. Although we had tremendous enthusiasm and support, the key problem was the ultimate sale to the end user. The product was considered somewhat sophisticated and high in price ($4,000 to $5,000 in 1968), and it required time and patience on the part of the salesperson who had to wait for budgets to be approved by the public school systems. In addition, in the early 1960s the budgets for educational systems were at an all-time high for any products that would increase the capacity of students to learn. This drive for education was spearheaded by Sputnik. Americans were pulling out all of the stops in order to catch up with the Russians' space program. Our product hit the market when this fad was over. Here is another message: If you are going to develop an idea or product that is in style presently, you had better make sure that you get it to the marketplace before the fad diminishes.

This is further confirmation of the New Company Syndrome and Murphy's Law on a start-up.

6

PLANNING FOR THE CASH

You have determined that your new venture is feasible, and all stations are go. You must now undertake the significant project of assessing your financial needs, shoring up your financial resources, and successfully obtaining the debt financing that you require. These are the areas that we shall tackle in this chapter.

Undercapitalization in a small company's development is one of the major factors contributing to the 80% of small-business failures. The *Annual Report on Small Business in Ontario: The State of Small Business, 1988* indicates that 80% of all loans to small business are made through the chartered banks. Although other avenues for financing a small-business start-up exist, chartered banks seem to be the main support.

So the first person to approach for financing is your friendly banker. When it's time to negotiate bank financing, you can save yourself a lot of time and get a better deal if you first consider your loan from your banker's point of view. Then supply everything that you know he or she will require.

First of all, the banker probably has a pretty low opinion of small businesses. Unfortunately, such a prejudice would not be ungrounded: numerous surveys in the United States and Canada have identified the major problems of small businesses as undercapitalization, inadequate or unreliable financial records, poor management, and an unfamiliarity with financial matters among small-business owners. The bankers have read these studies.

In fact, a 1982 study entitled *Chartered Bank Financing of Small Business in Canada* confirmed the earlier survey results.* Fewer than 10% of the small-business files held by chartered banks contained cash-flow statements or financial-statement forecasts. In other words, bankers had been lending money to small-business owners on the basis of their personal assets (mainly their homes), not on sound financial information. The study severely criticized bankers for the lack of judgment evident in lending depositors' money to small-business owners who may or may not have developed a feasible venture. Without adequate financial information, a banker could not possibly evaluate a business venture properly.

The Canadian chartered banks realized the error of their ways when they sustained substantial losses as a result of small-business failures during the 1982 recession. Their current approach to the assessment of loan applications is much more rigorous and needs to be understood by any prospective owner considering bank financing.

What Your Banker Is Looking For — And Why

The bank's gross profit, or spread, on loans (the difference between the cost of funds and the interest earned) is generally about three percent. This means that on a loan of $100,000, the bank's annual gross profit is $3,000. If the banker makes thirty-three $100,000 loans, only one needs to turn bad (causing the bank to forfeit $100,000) to wipe out the bank's gross profit for that year on all thirty-three loans. Although the banker's job is to lend money and make a profit for the bank, he or she generally lives in a world of negative reinforcement. A banker is expected to make loans as part of the job—but make one bad one, and look out.

---

*Larry Wynant, James Hatch, Mary Jane Grant, *Chartered Bank Financing of Small Business in Canada* (London: The School of Business Administration, University of Western Ontario, 1982).

If you approach your banker without the proper marketing, operations, and financial information about your new venture, then you will probably not receive any consideration for financing. A fair number of bankers pass up seemingly worthwhile loan applications if they are not presented in a proper manner. And that means a comprehensive, concise report on the venture, with *all* relevant financial information, in a single package commonly known as a business plan. A banker does not need (and will not tolerate) the annoyance of several phone calls to collect the details needed to support a loan of, say, $100,000, for an annual gross profit of $3,000. In short, the less time required by the banker to finalize your loan application, the more chance you have of receiving a yes.

In general terms, the banker has three basic criteria for measuring a good loan: 1. evidence of good management; 2. financial commitment; and 3. outside support.

Evidence of Good Management

Your record of strong management abilities in past business ventures and your experience in the industry or related businesses will be of great assistance to prove your good management ability. However, the banker will be measuring your management ability on the content and the manner in which you present your business plan. The emphasis here is on *your*. The business plan, which we shall discuss in detail shortly, must be prepared *by you*, with the possible assistance of a financial or marketing consultant. It should always be your plan, not theirs.

Many prospective small-business owners have gone to their accountants, thrown out some vague figures, and had the details processed by the accountant's computer, with the accountant making many of the key assumptions. Don't fall into that trap: you must understand every part of your business plan. You, not your accountant, must present these financial details to your banker with the total confidence that will come only from a complete understanding of, and commitment to, the plan.

Financial Commitment

Financial commitment is a true barometer of your commitment to your venture. In other words, how much have *you* got on the line? The equity you have invested in the company will be documented in the cash-flow projection (Exhibit 13) of your business plan where you will show your investment as the owner. (We previously suggested that your investment can be put into the company as a note instead of capital stock. Because bankers prefer your investment to be locked in, they will request that you sign an agreement that this note payable to you cannot be released without the prior agreement of the banker.) If you are purchasing a business, bankers usually like to see a debt-to-equity ratio of one to one—that is, the total liabilities, including bank loan, are equal to the equity invested in the company by you, the owner. However, they will consider a debt-to-equity ratio of, say, three to one, provided there are company assets to support the loan; namely accounts receivable and inventory. They will also require some outside support.

The total amount of an operating loan is usually a maximum amount that you will have access to. However, at any time during the year, the amount of the operating loan that you can use is based on the good receivables (under 90 days), the good inventory, and the value of equipment. It is common for the line of credit to be a certain amount, but it is subject to a maximum of 75% of the good accounts receivable, 50% of good inventory, and possibly 50% to 70% of good equipment. For example, let's assume that the operating loan or line of credit is $200,000.

Line of Credit		$200,000
Good receivables	$100,000 × 75%	$75,000
Good Inventory	$50,000 × 50%	$25,000
Equipment	$50,000 × 50%	$25,000
Maximum Bank will Allow		$125,000

Some small-business owners find themselves in difficulty after they have arranged a line of credit of, say, $200,000 yet find that the bank will only allow them to go to $125,000 because their good receivables are not adequate to support the bank loan. The bank refers to these terms as "margining."

Outside Support

Like it or not, on a start-up you should be prepared to sign a personal guarantee and possibly a collateral mortgage on your home. This is indeed a frightening prospect to many entrepreneurs. Obviously, you should try to negotiate a loan without a personal guarantee, but this will be very difficult without a strong financial commitment and a good debt-to-equity ratio on the balance sheet. The personal guarantee can become a stumbling block, as your spouse will be required to co-sign it. In some circumstances, a spouse may be unwilling to co-sign. If your spouse agrees, then he or she must receive independent legal advice.

Personal financial support means that you have personal assets such as a house, cottage, life insurance, marketable securities, or gold bricks that can be pledged to provide a backstop to the banker in case a financial problem arises that cannot be supported by your commitment on the balance sheet.

During the 1970s, banks focused on financial commitment and personal assets in their lending decisions; today, the emphasis is on good management. In other words, you must demonstrate to the banker that you are a good manager. You must develop a good business plan that confirms the feasibility of the venture. If you have a solid commitment to the new venture (debt-to-equity of one to one), then it is possible that you can establish reasonable borrowings for the new venture without having substantial personal assets or providing a personal guarantee.

The Business Plan

The business plan is mandatory for the success of *any* start-up, whether on the purchase of a business or franchise, whether financing is required or not. A business plan should be prepared at least once a year by all small-business owners to help attain personal and business goals.

A business plan consists of the following elements:

- a narrative report of two to three pages in length
- an operational plan (Exhibit 10)
- forecast monthly income statement (Exhibit 12)
- forecast monthly cash-flow statement (Exhibit 13)
- a copy of the latest financial statements signed by a chartered accountant if you are purchasing a company
- a personal net-worth statement
- a summary of borrowing requirements.

The narrative report describes the nature of the operation and the marketing approach, offers comments on the personnel and the structure of the company, and provides relevant details about the industry. It is essentially a summary of the details accumulated for your market analysis and feasibility study (Chapter 5).

The financial information required for the business plan is a statement forecasting monthly income and a statement forecasting monthly cash-flow for the following year. However, it is also a good idea to include other financial information that will be informative to the banker, such as sales by product grouping and some of the key operating ratios (described in Chapter 10) to demonstrate to the banker that you are aware of the financial details of your new business.

If you are buying a business or a franchise, you should also include some of the historic financial data for the operation, such as the recent financial statements (signed by a chartered accountant), calculations of some of the key ratios, and a summary of the adjustments to the income statement that you made in calculating indicated earnings as discussed in valuing the business, Chapter 4.

You should also include a personal net worth statement setting out the list of your personal assets and liabilities.

The Operational Plan

The first step in preparing your business plan is to develop your operational plan, which is a summary of the first year's operation for a start-up or the next year if you are purchasing a business. In effect, this is the foundation of your business plan. It is a follow-up from your feasibility study, as described in Chapter 5.

Operational planning can be broken down into the following five steps:

1. Assemble Information

The first step is to gather and organize the information developed in your feasibility study. This will include estimated sales by product group, calculation of gross profit, and the details of the operating expenses. This basic information must be supplemented with your knowledge of the industry including the market, competitors, suppliers, industry trends, and so forth. You also need information regarding the general economic climate, political events that could conceivably impact on the industry labor, and so forth.

List your competitors by name and estimated sales or market share. Compare details of your product or service with your competitors, considering price, delivery, quality, et cetera.

Based on the market analysis conducted in Chapter 5, and the other information gathered above, you should determine the size of the market and whether it is growing or shrinking. For example, fewer babies are being born and this could mean a long-term decline in that market area. On the other hand, "gray power" is increasing and demographics are swinging to those over sixty-five. Based on all of this information, you must decide the major factors that would influence either an upturn or downturn in the expected life-cycle of your product, your service, or the business you are about to start up or purchase.

List potential customers by size as well as order of importance.

Financial information was gathered in developing your feasibility study in Chapter 5. If you are buying a business or franchise, then review the historic financial data, particularly sales and gross profit by product group, collection rate of accounts receivable, labor costs, and all other relevant financial information. This fact-gathering exercise will provide you with the information you need to perform an informed analysis. It is the basis on which you will establish the ultimate business plan.

2. Analyze Information

Now you must analyze the information gathered. From it, you should determine the kinds of indicators or yardsticks that can measure where you stand in the industry. You should also determine what obstacles or problems stand in the way of achieving your goals. The key question is to determine what must be accomplished to make the plan happen and what the alternatives are. From this analysis, you should end up with a to-do list which should be narrowed down and transformed into specific routine objectives for the first year.

3. Establish Action Plans

Overall goals have now been clarified and you are beginning to build a picture of the results required for the first year to meet these goals. Objectives should be tied to specific periods of time; for example, months. What you want to achieve in the first year should be outlined in detail. You may also have longer-term goals which will be discussed later.

Focus primarily on those goals or objectives that will produce the highest results at the lowest cost and that are the most feasible and practical, and work out their optimal timing.

Having established objectives, the next step is to create a plan for each goal.

For example, one key goal is to attain the sales necessary to at least break even or make a reasonable profit. If the sales objective is say, $300,000 for the first year, then review the product lines and the specific target customers to determine which customer will be more receptive to buying the higher-margin products in your lines. In other words, list your potential customers on a spreadsheet with separate columns for the various products that you may be selling. Based on the information gathered, estimate what sales by product can be made to these individual clients during the first year. Although this may strike you as impossible, it is not; and by establishing these short-term goals and taking the necessary action, you are developing a strategy which will be your blueprint for success.

Your action plan must include details of the personnel

requirements: what employees will be hired, at what time during the first year, and what is the anticipated remuneration. The next major cost is the occupancy cost. The amount of space to be rented and the estimated cost per square foot, together with the utilities, property taxes, and maintenance costs must be summarized for the first year. You should now review the other operating expenses from your feasibility study conducted in Chapter 5 and adjust, either increasing or decreasing, the amounts based on the information gathered.

Remember, however, that a plan is not cast in stone. It must be flexible. Once you have put the plan into action, continue to accumulate detailed ongoing information to monitor its progress and to make the necessary alterations to cope with reality. Monitoring the plan will be dealt with in Chapter 10.

4. Detail the Operational Plan

It is now time to summarize these plans in the form of an income statement. The totals of the sales and the various expenses for wages, occupancy, and general expenses should be summarized for the year (See Exhibit 9: Operational Plan A.) Let us assume that this is a start-up of a wholesale company that is selling products with a gross profit average of about 30%. Let's further assume that the wages include the owner ($50,000), salesperson ($30,000), office staff ($25,000), and employee benefits ($5,000), for a total of $110,000. The space required, combining warehouse and office, is 2,500 square feet at $6.00 per foot (gross) or $15,000. Other expenses amount to $40,000. These other expenses are mainly advertising (say, $10,000), delivery using a subcontractor ($10,000), office expenses, and other miscellaneous items ($20,000). All this forecasts a net profit of $15,000.

At this point, you must review Plan A to determine if it meets your personal and business goals. Is it feasible?

5. Review the Plan

If Plan A does not meet your personal and business goals, you have to go back to the drawing board. This means reviewing the assembled information, reevaluating the analysis of

EXHIBIT 9

OPERATIONAL PLAN A
WHOLESALER INC.

Sales	$600
Gross Profit (30%)	180
Wages	110
Occupancy	15
Other	40
Total	165
Net Profit	$ 15

the information, and establishing new action plans. Let's assume that in this analysis you discover that some of the potential key customers establish their source of suppliers at the industry trade show.

With this new information, you may wish to alter your plan by increasing the marketing costs to include the industry trade show. You may also suggest that possibly a sales representative could be hired in the seventh month and not in the first month, as you would attract sales through the industry trade show without necessarily having a full-time sales representative on board. Your re-evaluation may suggest that you can increase your selling price by 5% with little or no reduction in the anticipated unit sales. Let's look at Plan B (Exhibit 10). Sales have increased from $600,000 to $630,000 (plus 5%) with a corresponding increase of gross profit to $210,000. Gross profit percentage has now increased from 30% to 33-1/3%. Wages have been reduced from $110,000 to $95,000 by delaying the hiring of the salesperson. Occupancy costs remain the same. Other expenses are increased by $5,000 due to the additional cost of attending the industry trade show. This results in an increased planned profit from $5,000 to $55,000. Let us now assume that Plan B is acceptable to the entrepreneur.

EXHIBIT 10

OPERATIONAL PLAN B
WHOLESALER INC.

Sales	$630
Gross Profit (33-1/3%)	210
Wages	95
Occupancy	15
Other	45
Total	155
Net Profit	$ 55

The final step is to review the details of your operational plan with your accountant or financial advisor, and one of your colleagues who has good marketing skills. What you want from these two individuals is hard objective, constructive criticism of your detailed plan and the resulting operational plan. After this, you should be able to finalize the operational plan for the first year of the company's operation.

Forecast Monthly Income and Cash-Flow Statements
Now it is time to convert the first year's operational plan into a forecast monthly income statement for the first twelve months. This is, in effect, the forecast of the sales, cost of sales, gross profit, and the expenses that will be incurred each month for the first year. This will be described later. After that, you are then required to prepare a forecast monthly cash-flow statement for the initial twelve-month period.

Many nonfinancial people confuse these two essential documents. The forecast monthly income statement projects the sales to be billed and the expenses to be incurred. The forecast monthly cash-flow statement represents the flow of cash coming in and going out of the company. For example, sales will be billed in month one, but the cash may not be collected until month two or three.

Similarly, you will purchase inventory in month one, but not pay for it until month three, for example. It is possible that some of the inventory purchased in month one may not even be shipped or sold to a customer until month four. Consequently, the cash for this inventory will have been expended in month three, but will not be billed to the customer until month four, and the cash may not be received until, say, month six.

The major importance of the forecast monthly income statement is to allow you to monitor the progress of your new business each month for the first twelve months. The main purpose of the monthly cash-flow statement is to provide you with the detailed cash requirements to finance the business. As indicated above, one of the major reasons for failures is inadequate financing or undercapitalization. In many cases, the small-business owner (a nonentrepreneur) did not have control, did not have the forecast monthly cash-flow report, and ultimately ran out of money.

In the past, many of these monthly forecasts were prepared manually for typing. Well, the technology era and the computer are here. In fact, a survey by one of the national Canadian banks indicated that sixty-five percent of small-business operations now have PCs or other computers. There are also numerous software programs that are available for processing the details of monthly forecasts (for example Lotus, Visicalc, and so forth). As over fifty percent of start-ups are made by individuals with post-secondary degrees, I assume that most of these individuals have or have access to a PC. They are aware of the spreadsheet programs that can be used to do the number crunching. If not, your accountant will be able to do this for you after you provide the basic assumptions.

Computerized forecasts will assure you of accurate figures. (The assumptions won't necessarily be accurate, though.) The forecast monthly income statement is automatically coordinated with the forecast monthly cash-flow statement and automatically produces a monthly balance sheet. The flexibility of using computerized spreadsheets for this purpose will allow you very simply and quickly to test "what if" scenarios. In other words, if you wish to change the projection to reflect increased or decreased selling prices, the resulting monthly forecasts will be processed very quickly. This will provide you with additional information to make informed decisions about all aspects of the venture.

Before this can be completed, you must summarize your operational plan and determine the basic assumptions for your monthly forecast income and cash-flow statements. The assumptions are merely details of the plan converted to common denominator dollars. Exhibit 10, which is Plan B, is the basis for the assumptions for the forecast monthly income statement. The main category for occupancy and other expenses should be broken down in finer detail. For example, occupancy includes rent, property taxes, repairs and maintenance, and utilities. Other expenses for a wholesale operation will include cartage or delivery, insurance, promotion or advertising, vehicle expenses, professional fees, office expenses, telephone, and so forth.

The following is an example of a basic assumption that would be made in preparing the forecast monthly income statement:

1. Sales by months for the year (give particular attention to peak and slack periods in the year). See Exhibit 11. Every industry is different. You must determine the seasonal trends of the industry of your choice. For example, many retailers find that November, December, and January account for 50% of annual sales due to Christmas and post-Christmas sales. Some industries will have higher sales during the months where the season changes, such as December and June. Most industries do have these trends, and you must determine them before you can complete your bills by months.
2. Estimated cost of sales percentage: 66-2/3%.
3. Breakdown of the expenses for wages (one-sixth of $80,000 for each of the first six months and one-sixth of $110,000 for each of the last six months) and occupancy (one-twelfth of $15,000). Other expenses must be estimated for the specific months. In many cases, it is simple and reasonably practical to divide the other expenses by twelve and allocate them to the individual months, realizing of course, that this will not be 100 percent accurate. However, when

you realize that there is a large expenditure of $5,000 for a trade show and it happens in, say, March, then it may be appropriate to allocate $5,000 to March and to divide the remainder of the other expenses of $40,000 equally among each of the twelve months. However, the more accurate you can be with allocating these expenses to the specific months, the more accurate your cash planning will be.

4. An interest factor on debt financing needs to be determined and this can be anywhere from 1% to 3% above prime or even higher. We will assume a rate of 15% per annum. For those companies expecting to be profitable in the first year, an income-tax calculation is also required. The corporate income tax rate for a small business on profits up to $200,000 per year is 22%.

EXHIBIT 11

FORECAST SALES BY MONTH
WHOLESALER INC.

Month

1	$ 10
2	20
3	30
4	40
5	50
6	50
7	50
8	60
9	60
10	80
11	90
12	90
TOTAL	$630

The following are the assumptions required for the forecast monthly cash-flow statement. Remember, this report is an estimate of the cash flow for your business.

1. All sales are collected in 45 days.
2. Inventory is purchased the month before it's sold and is paid for in 60 days.
3. All expenses are pro-rated on the basis of the monthly forecast income statement.
4. Rent paid in the first month is double, because it includes the last month's rent.
5. Warehouse equipment is purchased and paid for in the first month: $30,000.
6. Initial inventory purchase is $50,000.
7. Cash investment from owner is $100,000.

Obviously, every start-up will have different start-up expenditures. Exhibit 12 sets out the forecast monthly income statement using the above assumptions. Exhibit 13 sets out the forecast monthly cash-flow statement. You will notice that the profit of $55,000 shown at the end of the year in Exhibit 12 is the same as the profit in Exhibit 10, Operational Plan B, except for the added expense of interest. This expense was calculated in the forecast monthly cash flow.

Borrowing Requirements

The last page of your business plan should set out the borrowing requirements for your business. You will notice in Exhibit 13, cash requirements increase dramatically as the sales increase. Bankers generally like splitting bank financing between "term" and "operating" loans (sometimes referred to as line of credit).

Term Loans and Operating Loans

Knowing the difference between an operating loan and a term loan can help you take better control of your new business's finances. Generally, the operating loan is used to finance current assets: accounts receivable and inventory. This loan should fluctuate throughout the year as inventory and accounts receivable levels change.

EXHIBIT 12

FORECAST INCOME STATEMENT: WHOLESALER INC.

($)

	January	February	March	April	May	June	July	August	September	October	November	December	Total
Sales	10,000	20,000	30,000	40,000	50,000	50,000	50,000	60,000	60,000	80,000	90,000	90,000	630,000
Cost of sales	6,660	13,320	19,980	26,680	33,300	33,300	33,300	40,020	40,020	53,360	60,030	60,030	420,000
Gross profit	3,340	6,680	10,020	13,320	16,700	16,700	16,700	19,980	19,980	26,640	29,970	29,970	210,000
Expenses													
Wages	6,666	6,666	6,666	6,666	6,667	6,667	9,167	9,167	9,167	9,167	9,167	9,167	95,000
Occupancy	1,250	1,250	1,250	1,250	1,250	1,250	1,250	1,250	1,250	1,250	1,250	1,250	15,000
Other	3,333	3,333	8,333	3,333	3,333	3,333	3,333	3,333	3,334	3,334	3,334	3,334	45,000
Interest	0	0	0	166	246	286	284	251	217	204	129	95	1,879
Total expenses	11,249	11,249	16,249	11,415	11,496	11,536	14,034	14,001	13,968	13,955	13,880	13,846	156,879
Net profit	(7,909)	(4,569)	(6,229)	1,905	5,204	5,164	2,666	5,979	6,012	12,685	16,090	16,124	53,121

EXHIBIT 13

FORECAST CASH FLOW: WHOLESALER INC.
($)

	January	February	March	April	May	June	July	August	September	October	November	December	Total	
Cash Receipts														
Accounts receivable														
Opening	0	10,000	25,000	40,000	55,000	70,000	75,000	75,000	85,000	90,000	110,000	130,000	0	
Sales	10,000	20,000	30,000	40,000	50,000	50,000	50,000	60,000	60,000	80,000	90,000	90,000	630,000	A
Collections	0	5,000	15,000	25,000	35,000	45,000	50,000	50,000	55,000	60,000	70,000	85,000	495,000	
Closing	10,000	25,000	40,000	55,000	70,000	75,000	75,000	85,000	90,000	110,000	130,000	135,000	135,000	
Investment	100,000												100,000	B
Cash Disbursements														
Payables														
Opening	50,000	63,320	33,300	46,660	59,980	66,600	66,600	73,320	80,040	93,380	113,390	120,060	50,000	
Purchases	13,320	19,980	26,680	33,300	33,300	33,300	40,020	40,020	53,360	60,030	60,030	60,030	473,370	
Payments	0	50,000	13,320	19,980	26,680	33,300	33,300	33,300	40,020	40,020	53,360	60,030	403,310	C
Closing	63,320	33,300	46,660	59,980	66,600	66,600	73,320	80,040	93,380	113,380	120,060	120,060	120,060	

	1	2	3	4	5	6	7	8	9	10	11	12	Total	
Expenses														
Wages	6,666	6,666	6,666	6,666	6,667	6,667	9,167	9,167	9,167	9,167	9,167	9,167	95,000	
Occupancy	2,500	1,250	1,250	1,250	1,250	1,250	1,250	1,250	1,250	1,250	1,250	1,250	16,250	
Other	3,333	3,333	8,333	3,333	3,333	3,333	3,333	3,333	3,334	3,334	3,334	3,334	45,000	
Warehouse equipment	30,000												30,000	
Interest				166	246	286	284	251	217	204	129	95	1,879	
	42,499	11,249	16,249	11,415	11,496	11,536	14,034	14,001	13,968	13,955	13,880	13,846	188,129	D
Cash Over/Short	57,501	(56,249)	(14,569)	(6,395)	(3,176)	164	2,666	2,699	1,012	6,025	2,760	11,124	3,561	E
Loan Beginning	0	57,501	1,252	(13,317)	(19,712)	(22,889)	(22,725)	(20,059)	(17,360)	(16,348)	(10,323)	(7,563)	0	
Loan	57,501	1,252	(13,317)	(19,712)	(22,889)	(22,725)	(20,059)	(17,360)	(16,348)	(10,323)	(7,563)	3,561	3,561	

$$*E = A + B - C - D$$

The term loan is used primarily to finance the purchase of fixtures, leasehold improvements, and other fixed assets whose value will not fluctuate, but will depreciate over time. For these items, it makes sense to borrow on a term basis, with a repayment schedule over three to twelve years, depending on the life of these capital assets. Bankers like term loans because repayment of principal is built into the financing package. Also, banks charge one-quarter to one-half percent higher interest on a term loan than on an operating loan.

There is more to a bank term loan than meets the eye, however. The term loan from a finance company for your automobile, for example, is payable over the term of the loan, if you are not in default. As a result, you only have to worry about keeping payments up to date. A term loan from a bank is tied into your operating loan.

Most bank term-loan agreements include several covenants. In addition to keeping payments up to date, for example, you might have to keep key balance sheet ratios in line and restrict payments to yourself or partners. Usually any amounts advanced by you to the company require the permission of the bank before you can be repaid.

Although the term loan may be signed up for a period of ten years, the banker can call it if you do not adhere to the specific details set out in the loan agreement. Term loans and operating loans can also be considered "demand loans." And the bank can call them at any time if they are unhappy with your performance.

The Small Business Loans Act

The term loan being used to finance the purchase of fixtures, leasehold improvements, and equipment may qualify under the Small Business Loans Act (SBLA). In simple terms, the SBLA allows you to borrow funds from a chartered bank at a preferred interest rate of prime plus 1%. (You can expect to pay up to prime plus 3% for your normal term loans.) Qualifying under the SBLA, then, can save some money for you. The reason that the banks are happy to loan you these funds under the SBLA is that they have a guarantee from the government of 85% of any of the losses that may occur.

This means that their risk is lower than for traditional loans. Loans under the SBLA are term loans and repayment terms are built in for a period of up to ten years. You may be quick to ask: "If the loans are guaranteed, then why doesn't the bank make all the loans they can?" According to the act, the loans must be made in the traditional manner and the chartered bank must rate the application as if no guarantee were available. In other words, you must present a bankable situation; that is, one where the banker is convinced that it is a good loan.

In addition, the banker realizes that there will be some administrative time necessary to oversee the loan during its term. With an annual profit of 3%, a banker is not quick to loan money to anyone who cannot demonstrate his or her ability to service the debt; in other words, pay principal and interest as stated in any banking agreement. Some bankers contend that the administration time alone eats up all of the gross profit on these loans. In addition, in the late 1980s, the government made it difficult for banks to collect on some of the guarantees by using the excuse that the paperwork did not have all the i's dotted and the t's crossed. As a result, your banker may not be especially happy to process a loan for you under the SBLA, but it is still to your advantage to apply and to benefit from the lower interest rate.

Finalizing and Presenting the Business Plan
You have now assembled all the elements of your business plan, as described on p. 86. All the material should be bound in a suitable folder for presentation to the banker. But before you contact the banker, it is also worthwhile to have your financial consultant or accountant and your marketing advisor review the details for any last-minute changes. To repeat, if you are purchasing a franchise or a business, then the business plan should include the last two years' financial statements signed by a chartered accountant and financial information provided by the franchiser.

It is now time to seek out the banker you wish to deal with. Do not be influenced by the many horror stories you have heard about the various banks in the past few years. Make enquiries of your friends, associates, and industry association personnel as to who is a good banker. In the long run, you are dealing with an individual, not an institution. Don't make the mistake of automatically going to the banker who looks after your personal affairs. It is important that you deal with a banker in a commercial center who understands small-business commercial banking. They can be very helpful in providing you with guidance as to any possible shortcomings in your business plan. You can also expect some pointed questions which may require additional research on your part.

Once you have decided on the banker, then it is time to dial his or her number and set up an appointment. It is a good idea to send the banker your business plan at least one to two days in advance of your meeting.

At the meeting, it is important that *you* present *your business plan* to the banker. You may wish to take along your financial consultant or accountant as a backstop, but under no circumstances should this person be anything more than support. This is when you put your best foot forward to demonstrate to the banker that you are a good manager. In addition to presenting your business plan, you should have any other visual information that will enhance your presentation: brochures, pictures, demonstration kit, or even a video. Your banker is a busy person. Keep your meeting to twenty or thirty minutes.

Your Relationship with the Bank

Let's say you have made a good presentation and you acquire the proper financing for your business. Down the road, you may require additional financing to fund expansions. It is important, therefore, that you maintain a good relationship with your banker from the outset. Your banker should think of you as a good manager. Here are some basic tips:

1. Don't exceed your operating limit.
2. Take the time to bring your banker up to date on where your company stands. Don't play ostrich and hide your head in the sand when problems arise. This results in a breakdown in communications. One of the major keys to a good bank relationship is communication.

3. Get a handle on your bank position. Keep a daily summary of cheques issued and deposits made. Calculate your bank balance daily. When you expect to be over your operating loan limit, pick up the phone and tell your banker, explaining the circumstances before you issue the cheques. He or she won't like it, but if forewarned and brought up to date, then chances are good the cheques will pass.

   This will put you in what is referred to as an overdraft position. This can present a double whammy. First your banker is generally unhappy with this, and it may curtail your financing in the years to come. Second, the interest charge can be as high as 7% or 8% over the bank prime rate.

4. Get to know exactly what is happening by having financial statements prepared on a monthly basis. They will not guarantee a profitable business, but you will know the state of your company's health. It will give you a fix on where you stand and how the actual progress compares to your business plan. It is a good idea to give a copy of the monthly statement to your banker. If the statement indicates that things are not going as well as they should, let the banker know what you are doing about it.

5. Make sure that your monthly accounts receivable lists and inventory certificates are taken to the bank as soon as possible after the month-end. You will have agreed to this when you received approval for your bank loan. Maintaining your position as a good manager means following up on any commitments that you have made to your banker.

Open lines of communication with your banker can reap many dividends. His or her experience can be very helpful when you are called on to make important decisions. Your banker can be a very useful sounding board and a key support to your finance leg.

Alternative Sources of Financing
Let's look at alternative methods of financing. The first place to look is at yourself. It is fair to say that you won't get your new venture off the ground without having some of your own cash. Dehired middle managers will have received the golden

handshake and, no doubt, accumulated some personal assets in the form of a home and possibly some investments in Canada Savings Bonds and so forth. I realize that many people do not wish to jeopardize their home when starting a business. But remember, to buy yourself a job, you need some of your own money. However, in many cases, this is the major asset that can be used to finance the start-up. It can be used in a few ways. You can mortgage up to 75% of the market value. For example, if your home is valued at $200,000 and you have a current mortgage of $25,000, then the total mortgage could be $150,000 or an additional $125,000. You can remortgage to obtain the $125,000 to put into the business or you can provide what is called a collateral mortgage to a lending institution to support the company's borrowings. If you have Canada Savings Bonds or other marketable securities, then you should either cash them in or pledge them to the bank for security on your bank borrowings. I suggest they be cashed in to increase your "commitment" to the business.

If your personal assets and your own cash are not adequate to provide the lending institution with the necessary "commitment," then another idea is to approach friends or relatives for what is commonly called "love money." This can come in the form of a personal loan to you or to your company or possibly the purchase of some common or preferred shares. Before you approach any of your good friends or relatives, have your business plan completed so that you have full confidence in the success of your new venture. You do not need the worry of losing the money of individuals whom you must deal with for the remainder of your life. If any of your good friends or relatives really like you, they will not commit any funds to your company without reviewing your business plan.

Another source of financing is employees. That is, of course, if you have any. This is a double benefit in that you may obtain some of the necessary capital required to start the business and, in addition, you will have motivated employees who will be more than interested in seeing the venture succeed. The problem, of course, is that they may consider themselves partners and try to get involved in the day-to-day management of your new venture.

You may wish to commence the venture with a partner who cannot only provide some of the upfront seed capital, but can also complement your skills and help to bolster one of the legs of the management tripod. I am sure that you have heard many of the partnership horror stories. Well, for every horror story, there are many partnerships that have proven successful. The secret is to get the right partner and do the paperwork upfront. The paperwork means the shareholders' agreement which should spell out the manner in which the partnership will operate. The agreement will deal with the transfer of shares, the death of a shareholder, the physical disability of a shareholder, and the termination or retirement of a shareholder. But this agreement is only a small part of the total. Your partner must be compatible, complement your skills, and provide a necessary part of the management team.

The Federal Business Development Bank, which is an agency of the federal government, is another source to consider. They have been referred to as the "lender of last resort." It is possible that if you are turned down by a chartered bank, that the Federal Business Development Bank will consider your loan or be able to facilitate it with their matchmaking procedures and venture capital program. To obtain more detailed information on the matchmaking procedures of the FBDB, you should call the local regional office for specific details on how you might apply. Some complain that the FBDB's interest rates are higher than the chartered banks. However, the fact remains that the most important part of starting up is getting the money and the extra one-half percent on $100,000 represents $500 per year. If this extra amount jeopardizes the success of your venture, then you shouldn't start at all.

Another way to finance a start-up is to lease any of the fixed assets required for the business. Leasing provides two main advantages. First, you are only required to pay out the first and last months' lease cost, and second, the interest rate is locked in. In other words, once you sign the lease, the payments are locked in for the term of the lease. Any fluctuations of the interest rates upwards will not affect your costs. The lease financing is not tied in with the chartered bank. As long as you are not in default with payments, no one can call the "loan." The only disadvantage is that the interest rates built into the leasing costs will be a little higher than the traditional banking rates, but this can be a small price to pay in order to establish the proper financing for your new business.

In some situations, it is possible to finance inventory by purchasing the product on a consignment basis or on floor-plan financing, which means that you pay nothing for the product until it is sold. In the case of consignment, the manufacturers may be happy to deal in this way at no additional cost for interest or finance charges. However, floor plans, which are financed by third-party financing companies, will usually charge interest at a few points over prime for the cost of the items. This is usually only common in retail operations where the manufacturer or wholesaler is anxious to get a product line displayed and in front of the end user.

Suppliers can be a source of financing. In addition to floor plans and inventory on consignment, you can also negotiate payment terms. This is usually a problem for a start-up venture, but there is no harm trying. And it is something to keep in mind for the future. Some suppliers may be happy to deliver an abnormally high quantity of a product with "dating" terms of payments in 90 days or more. This can go a long way to financing both your start-up inventory and your ongoing inventory requirements. However, it is important that you determine how long it will take to sell the product that you will be paying for in 90 days. If it is much longer than 90 days, then you may wish to reconsider, cut back the quantity, or negotiate 120 days.

Lately, a common source of financing is the personal credit cards of the aspiring entrepreneur. Granted, in some cases, the finance costs will be about 2% per month on the outstanding balance. But you have use of the funds. It may be the difference between success and failure, starting or not starting.

Everyone has heard of venture capital. Unfortunately, too

many small-business owners aspiring to start up are disappointed when they discuss their requirements with a venture capitalist. The venture capitalist normally will only consider loans of $500,000 to $1,000,000 minimum.

If you do get involved with a venture capitalist, and you are able to come to some terms, then you should understand how they operate. The right venture capital firm can provide you with much more than capital. Personnel may have expertise in your field. They can provide you with the management backup, the marketing information, and the know-how in your industry. This may assure the success of your project. However, there is a price. In talking to a venture capitalist, you will discover that for every ten investments, one is a real winner, two are pretty good, three are the living dead, and the remainder are losers. Because of the high risk, venture capitalists are usually looking for an annual return of about 25% to 50% or even higher.

Chapter 15 sets out more specific information on how to deal with venture capitalists.

7

HUMAN RESOURCES

Up to now, you have been working with paper, planning all phases of your new venture. You now have the idea, it's feasible, and you are happy with the business plan. Now it's time for action. There is no point getting the business (marketing leg) if you can't do the business (operations leg). No doubt you have run into many situations where fast-talking salespeople sell you on a product or service, but when the dust settles, they can't "deliver." Don't exaggerate the merits of your products or services. This is shortsighted and can spell disaster for the long-term profitability of your business.

To ensure the long-term success of any small business, you must be able to "deliver" the service or product. You must provide the service and the quality that is advertised or promised when you close the sale. In any business, but especially in the service business, your growth of new business will come from the referrals of your satisfied customers. In fact, one satisfied customer can cause your business to grow dramatically over the years if he or she refers another satisfied customer, who refers another satisfied customer, and so forth. Conversely, one dissatisfied customer in the first months of your business can result in the loss of many future possible customers. It has been suggested that one dissatisfied customer will tell ten to twelve people, whereas a satisfied customer will only tell four to six. The compounding effect of losing a potential ten to twelve customers who might have referred four to six in the future can be disastrous to your start-up and most certainly will curtail any chance of rapid growth.

There are three types of business owners: those who are reputable, those who are con men, and those who are frauds. Only the reputable will survive in the long run, and these are the people who "deliver."

Excellence in Small Business

This means that you need to set up an organization that will be here for the long term. This organization will want sales, but not the quick buck at the expense of the firm's reputation and long-term survival.

Thomas Peters and Robert Waterman, in their book, *In Search of Excellence*, outlined eight basic principles of excellence, demonstrated by the large firms that were successful in the 1970s. These bear repeating:

1. Bias for action versus paralysis by analysis.
2. Staying close to the customer.
3. Autonomy and entrepreneurship.
4. Productivity through people.
5. Hands-on, value driven.
6. Stick to the knitting.
7. Simple form, lean staff, few administrative layers.
8. Simultaneous loose-tight properties.

Although these are considered the qualities of excellence in a large firm, they are in fact the qualities characteristic of successful small businesses. In other words, the successful large firms are those that are able to manage and retain the qualities characteristic of a small business.

1. As a true entrepreneur, you will be able to make informed decisions very quickly without committees, head-office approval, or boards of directors.
2. You will know many of your customers personally, certainly in the initial stages. This should continue in the long run if you wish to maintain your title of entrepreneur.

3. You have autonomy automatically and, if you maintain control, you will have entrepreneurship as well.
4. Small business is people business. Your long-term success will be through the people you hire, train, supervise, and encourage to use their own entrepreneurial strengths.
5. As a small-business owner, you will keep in touch with detailed operations and be concerned about value for your clients and customers.
6. When you consider yourself a complete success, you may tend to think about the greener pastures over the hill. But a true entrepreneur will "stick to the knitting." True entrepreneurs avoid needless diversification to satisfy ego.
7. You will have few administrative layers and will have direct contact with all of the staff who work for you, certainly in the formative years. As a true entrepreneur, you will operate a lean machine.
8. Although the business schools try to convince everyone that every company, regardless of size, requires a hard-and-fast organizational chart, setting out everyone's responsibilities, authority, and so forth, you will probably follow the line of the excellent big companies by maintaining a simultaneously loose and tight management structure. In other words, your staff will know what is to be done, who is to do it, and when, without having a rigid formal structure.

It is also interesting to note that Peters and Waterman's complaints against management in the mediocre big firms included:

1. Managers do not take enough interest in people.
2. Top managers are isolated from staff.

As a true entrepreneur, you must be quick to recognize the value of the people whom you choose to represent your product or participate in providing your service. And recognizing their value, you must naturally stay closely involved with them, to understand their outlook, the problems they encounter, et cetera. In other words, you wear the hat of vice-president of human resources for your small business and in the long run your aim is to develop staff who can "deliver." They are the mainstay of your operation.

Hiring the Right Staff

A major problem for most small-business owners is hiring staff suitable for the various jobs. This is accentuated at start-up.

Take yourself for example. You have to wear many hats: vice-president of human resources, chief financial officer, vice-president of marketing, and general manager. You can't be good at all of these functions, but neither can you shirk responsibility for any of them.

Then, how do you get around this critical problem? The first thing is to look at the jobs for which you need people. For example, let's look at an example of a wholesale company that requires a salesperson and an office person, but can only afford one employee. The first step is to define each of the jobs. The next step is to prioritize the specific job functions. In other words, if you are looking for a Person Friday to handle the office, including opening mail, doing some book-keeping, answering the phone, filing, trouble-shooting, maintaining inventory records, ordering product, taking phone orders, answering customers' enquiries, and so forth, then you must determine which of these functions is the most important. To have the ideal employee for the various functions, you would probably need two to four people. But you can only afford one. The secret, then, is to determine the key function. If it happens to be maintaining inventory control and ordering product, then you will need someone who is cautious, practical, patient, and precise. You should hire someone with these personal traits. Unfortunately, this person could lack some self-confidence, may not be outgoing, not necessarily quick, and may not be the type of person that would be ideally suited to taking phone orders, handling customer complaints, and generally dealing with your customers.

As productivity through people is the key to your ultimate success, you must hire carefully. No matter how hard it is to get good people, it is a lot more difficult and costly if you have to fire them later or if they quit because you misrepresented the job. Do your homework before attempting to recruit anyone. Know exactly the type of person you are looking for.

Learn to recognize the personality type of the people you consider for positions in your company. Several characteristics will go hand in hand in any given type. For example, some people are aggressive, assertive, self-confident, and adventurous, while others are cautious, helpful, considerate, and loyal. Some are outgoing, persuasive, enthusiastic, and optimistic, while others are reserved, direct, pessimistic, and secretive. Some are placid, passive, and easy-going, while others are nervous, impatient, and quick. Some people are dependent, precise, worriers, and respectful of authority, while others are independent, careless with detail, informal, and resistant to authority. Although degrees of each of these characteristics exist in each person, of course, you can detect a preponderance of similar traits and guess quite closely the personality type of a given person.

When you are considering any position for your new venture, you must first decide on the personality type required for that position. In other words, what personal characteristics should the employee have for the specific jobs? For example, if your product is highly technical and you require a salesperson who can deal with engineers or highly technical people in the customer's company, then you need someone who can talk their language and relate to their activity. An outgoing, aggressive person who is impatient and careless with detail will, no doubt, have difficulty relating to these people. This person is not likely to provide good results. In the long-run, your customer will probably have more confidence in someone who is more low-key, helpful, direct, easy-going, and precise. On the other hand, if you have a consumer product that requires a self-starter to knock on doors and be a strong "closer," then the aggressive, out-going person will probably fit the bill.

There are many sources of employees. You can simply ask your friends or business associates if they know anyone who meets your requirements. If you are forced to advertise, then be sure you select the right medium. Usually the best approach is through small local papers because the cost of advertising is lower and the readership is concentrated in your area. Take time to prepare an ad that will present the information that you feel necessary and appealing: the type of job, the location, the salary and benefits, and the company's name (this is a backhand way of advertising). Some individuals looking for a job are reluctant to reply to box numbers in case it is their own company that is advertising. Some experts suggest that the days to advertise are Tuesday, Wednesday, and Thursday. You should probably let the ad run for at least three days.

Interviewing and Recruiting

If your advertisement includes a telephone number (which is usually best), then you should have a telephone interview form in order to screen the applicants before making an appointment for a personal interview that could be a waste of time. Key information to be gleaned from the telephone interview includes, of course, name and telephone number; whether the person is working now and when he or she would be available; what his or her experience and education are; current salary; why he or she is leaving; and other details that you feel necessary to determine the extent of the person's experience and his or her compatibility with your company.

After you have reviewed the telephone interviews, then contact the individuals you wish to interview personally. Before you conduct any interviews, review the details of the job, the skills or knowledge you require, and the personality you are looking for. It is also a good idea to have specific questions that you wish to ask in order to bring out the personality of the person being interviewed. In addition, get an application form completed and determine the practical tests that will be used to confirm any of the comments. For example, you may need a typing test, a word-processor test, or a quiz to check the applicant's knowledge of computers and software programs (ACCPAC, Lotus, and so forth).

Before asking any questions, describe the job in detail. Be sure the person knows what they will have to do all day and how their work will be judged. Bend over backwards to be honest and truthful in explaining what the job really consists of. In other words, there are always pros and cons to any job; make certain that the individual knows what the drawacks are (without, of course, exaggerating them). You should have a salary or wage in mind, and this should be communicated to the interviewee along with the hours and the benefits. This may eliminate many applicants, and you will not have to bother continuing any further.

If the applicant is still interested, then ask the questions you have written down. Applicants seldom lie, but they often exaggerate.

If you have several people to interview for the job, then it is appropriate to evaluate the interviewee after each interview by using the matrix problem-solving approach. Very simply, list across the top of a sheet of paper the qualities you are looking for. They can include neatness, computer skills, cautiousness versus aggressiveness, an outgoing personality versus an introverted one, impatience versus patience, precision versus independence, and so forth. Your questions should be designed to allow you to evaluate each of these items. On completion of the interview, I suggest you rank it on a scale of 1 to 5; 1 for Poor and 5 for Good.

On completion of all interviews, an academic evaluation of the interviewees would indicate that you should hire the applicant with the highest score. But before you make an academic decision, you should reevaluate the applicants who may be ranked second and third and review your decision.

Before you finalize your decision, check references. Your key questions should pertain to skills and personality. Other questions might include the following: Was the candidate conscientious, punctual, personable, and competent on the job? Did he or she exhibit any personality problems or reluctance to follow directions? Why did he or she leave? Did the applicant have a good attitude? A key final question: Would you rehire the applicant?

Remember, it is very expensive to hire the wrong person. The costs of advertising, interviewing, and paying, say, the first three months salary, only to discover that you've hired the wrong person can be costly. However, this is the tip of the iceberg. The hidden cost is the possible loss of current customers and future customers if your employee is wrong for the job.

You may wish to use some personnel tests to confirm your evaluation of the applicants. Although many people have mixed emotions about industrial psychologists, you may wish to engage one to review your top two or three candidates. I agree that this can be costly, but in the long run, it is probably a great deal less costly than hiring the wrong person.

One major mistake is under- or over-hiring. If you hire someone who is under-qualified, the result may be poor performance of the job. If you over-hire, the employee will leave when he or she gets bored—a couple of months later.

If you find that your ad has attracted no applicants, or inadequate applicants, then you may be forced to use the services of a professional employment agency. This too can be costly. However, it will save you considerable time, and remember, your time is money.

Training and Motivating Your Staff
Most entrepreneurs are optimistic and enthusiastic. When the right person is hired, they sometimes assume that the new employee can do the job immediately. This assumption couldn't be further from the truth. Don't expect new employees to jump right in and perform a job comparable to what you have been doing. You must be patient (and you probably aren't), spend time showing your new employee what to do, and explain exactly what the jobs are and the manner in which they should be done. On-the-job training is far superior to classroom training. If you are the boss, then you are the teacher. Remember, adults learn by doing, not by watching and listening. This teaching deserves a fair share of your time; it will build up your business so that you can "deliver."

Now that you have the right employees, you must handle them properly. You can be sure of one thing. When your employees were hired, they intended to do a good job. Assuming that your employees have the necessary skills and personality, the only reason they have been discouraged from the job is because of you, the owner. In other words, they are demotivated.

Now that you have bought your own job and you are your own boss, you will have problems you never dreamed of. The majority of your problems will revolve around people; namely your people. Remember Harry Truman's expression: "The buck stops here." When you have people problems, the odds are that the converse is true: "The buck starts here." There is a good chance that the majority of your people problems will have been created by you. Handle or motivate your staff properly, and you will minimize your problems and sleepless nights and maximize your bottom line. Job satisfaction is cited as the most important factor for motivating employees. Some suggest that if you avoid discouraging your staff and pay well, there really isn't anything else needed to motivate them. You demotivate and discourage employees when you violate the rules of ordinary courtesy: bawl them out in front of other employees; over-supervise; play favorites; and generally beat people down.

Remember how you felt as an employee. No doubt you thought you needed a ten percent raise but realized you were likely to continue on at the same rate. Well, your employees feel the same way. If your memory serves you correctly, you will also realize that nonfinancial rewards are really all your previous employer could offer in addition to a reasonable wage.

What are some of the nonfinancial rewards? You will find an employee feels good and works better when he or she has been given some recognition. Providing a good atmosphere for work and informing employees about both good and bad developments in business can be two steps in the right direction. John Naisbitt, in his book *Megatrends*, suggests that trends start from the bottom up and fads from the top down. Your employees on the line may be able to provide you with some good input as to the company's operation. It's a good idea to ask employees questions. You may be surprised to find out that they are doing something that is unnecessary or not doing something that is necessary. The key, however, is to listen to the answer and possibly follow up with another question to prove that you were listening. On occasion, it is a good idea to give an employee a pat on the back. This can be the greatest nonfinancial reward you can bestow on a member of your staff.

Another key element in motivating staff is, perhaps, to

fire the drones. Good workers do not like to see incompetence around them. Although you need people to fill the various functions in the company, the wrong person will be costly and will also disrupt the other employees. Don't tolerate troublemakers or nonperformers. Get rid of them immediately.

The Labor Acts from the various provinces set out the minimum separation allowance on the termination of any employee. However, the 1980s saw numerous lawsuits by disgruntled ex-employees who sued their previous employers for wrongful dismissal. If an employee was in a management role of any sort, or if he or she had a title, such as sales manager, operations manager, or office manager, then you could consider paying something in excess of the Provincial Labor Law. Prior to dismissal, it is important that you document your discussions with the employee, setting out the details of his or her inadequacies in the position that he or she held. Without this documentation and without action on your part prior to terminating employment, you may very easily find yourself being sued for wrongful dismissal.

A financial incentive to employees is generally received with mixed emotions. Setting up rewards can be a tricky proposition and in the long run could provide negative motivation for your staff. An example is an incentive program based on profits. Let's assume one of the key employees receives a bonus at year-end of $5,000. Whether you like it or not, that employee has registered this amount as part of his or her remuneration for the job. If next year, the bonus is $1,000, then you have created a problem that did not exist before the incentive program was implemented.

However, if an incentive program can be developed where the individual employee can measure exactly how the amount has been calculated and where he or she has full control of the performance, then this employee may be highly motivated by a cash incentive.

In the early years of my company, I established an incentive program for staff that would be paid out in June and in December. The total bonus was determined by the profits, after I had paid a reasonable salary to myself. The split among the employees was determined by their individual productivity, which in all cases was calculable, together with some discretionary valuations by myself. The staff were pleased to receive this bonus cheque before their summer holidays and before Christmas. At that time, eight bookkeepers were on the payroll, including students in registered programs for CGA and CMA. I was informed that my wage scale for these employees was somewhat lower than the going rate in the industry. However, the industry did not pay any bonuses. I asked the group if they would rather that I adjusted their pay to the bonus base and eliminated the bonus. The combination was higher than the going rate for the industry. There was a resounding yes. So much for the incentive program.

Each small business will be different. Anyone starting a small business should be very careful about how he or she implements any monetary incentives. I suggest that you pay the industry rate and motivate your people with nonfinancial rewards.

Expert Help

By now, you have discovered that you can't do justice to all facets of your business. Granted, you can handle the areas of your expertise, but you will require outside help to offset some of your weak areas. Believe it or not, your number one outside advisor is your accountant.

Your Accountant

According to a study published in the *Journal of Small Business Canada*, your accountant is your number one outside advisor, followed by your banker, lawyer, and consultant. This was confirmation of a similar study conducted in the United States.

Another study published by the *Journal of Commercial Lending* indicated that the reason for the financial failure of eighteen percent of the companies surveyed was incompetent accountants.

The message is clear. Some accountants are better at their profession than others. The fact is reflected again in the U.S. failure study, which reports forty-eight percent of failures resulted from incomplete accounting records. So if your accountant is going to be your number one adviser, you had better make sure that your accounting firm is on the ball. That means you need a third-wave accountant and not an old-fashioned second-wave "bean counter."

First of all, don't be intimidated by your accountant, accountant's jargon, and complicated reports. To set the record straight, try thinking of the accountant as just another major supplier. When ordering services and materials, you will be specifying the details of the requirements, such as price, date of delivery, or timing. The only difference is that your accountant is providing financial and accounting services. Before ordering, determine your needs, and get some idea of the price and delivery date.

Some accounting firms are only interested in preparing your year-end financial statements and your corporate tax records. Your accountant can and should do much more than just offer these services. A competent professional accounting firm can recommend basic control systems for cash, inventory, and accounts receivable. It should be able to provide a full range of advisory services, suggesting what monthly financial information you need. It should show you how to generate the information yourself or provide computerized financial information through the firm's own computers (or a service bureau).

You should feel comfortable about calling your accountant to discuss major problems and your decisions. Your accounting firm is an important partner in establishing bank credit, negotiating loan extensions or increases, making decisions about expansion or acquisition, and slimming down operations. But your accounting firm should be doing even more. Your accountant should help you with tax planning. This should be an integral part of most of your financial and business decisions. Profits don't mean much if you don't get to keep them. If you are looking to buy a business, you should be able to rely on your accounting firm for guidance, a realistic valuation of the business being purchased, and the best method of purchase.

Another important item on your shopping list is the bill. Most accountants charge by the hour. Usually, the bigger the accounting firm, the higher the rates. Rates can vary, depending on the staff member involved. (A junior in a major firm may slog away for $50 an hour while the senior partner may be charged out at $200 to $300 an hour.) However, the hourly rates really don't mean much. It is the total fee that counts and the dollars saved because of the advice. Some firms will act as an outside vice-president of finance or controller if they are paid a monthly retainer. The advantage of this system is that you're sure to get the attention you want, and the accounting firm will be following outside developments on your behalf. But again, don't expect Cadillac service at Chev prices. This is an area to watch closely, but not to scrimp on. While there's little you can do to distort the old adage that time is money, there are ways to minimize the total charge. The obvious one is to keep accurate bookkeeping records and maintain strict control systems. You will be paying excessive accounting fees if your accountants are required to perform mundane duties at the year-end to clean up a mess that could have been avoided by a properly trained bookkeeper who charges from $15 to $25 per hour. Needless to say, the low-tech days of the shoebox accounting system are long gone. With the Goods and Services Tax (GST) implemented on January 1, 1991, it is mandatory that all businesses, no matter how small, maintain impeccable records to be certain that they recover the GST tax paid on their purchases.

Another common mistake is to have a December 31 year-end. This date is probably the worst one you could choose. Accountants are faced with a deluge of December 31 year-ends. This can mean that the smaller the business, the lower the priority. The result, as usual, can be poor service for the little guy. It may be preferable to review your operations and choose a date that is at the slowest time of your business cycle and when inventory is at the lowest level. Or choose the slower time for accounting firms, between June and October. You might even be able to strike a deal on a special off-season fee.

Another way to save on accounting fees is to have unaudited instead of audited statements. Audited statements make bankers feel a little more comfortable and accounting firms a little richer, but they aren't always required. The major advantage of an unaudited financial report is that the accountants' fee can be up to fifty percent less.

How do you go about engaging the right accounting firm? Here are the steps you can take:

1. Know what services you need (monthly financial statements, advisory services, personal tax planning, year-end financial statements, and so forth).
2. Seek names of firms from your banker, lawyer, business associates, and your trade association.
3. Telephone two or more of the firms and make an appointment with the senior partner. Meet at their office. Note the facility, the number of partners, and the quality of staff.
4. Have the partner demonstrate the various services offered. Meet the partner involved in tax matters. See who is in charge of the bookkeeping function.
5. After the tour, sit down and briefly explain what services you need with what frequency. You have every right to expect the partner to give you a ballpark figure on the annual bill. Have him or her identify this in a letter of engagement. It will set out the full range of services provided and the estimated cost.
6. Don't always grab the low fee. You should be looking at the total estimated charge as it relates to the service you have outlined. It's a good idea to look for an accounting firm with small-business experience. Generally, accountants are trained in big-business theory, and some are unable to make the jump to the small business arena which is different. In other words, a small business is not a small big business. You do not want to be paying for training on the job. Remember, a good accounting firm can save more than the annual cost of the accounting services.

Your Banker

We have already discussed dealing with your banker in Chapter 6. But it is important to remember that your banker is touted as being your number two advisor. A banker can be a good friend if you wish to expand or if you find yourself in a downturn. Demonstrating your good management ability to your banker and maintaining strong communications is one of the most important elements of the future success of your business.

Your Lawyer

Let's look at your number three advisor: your lawyer. One of the costs of buying yourself a job is legal services. When you consider the proliferation of regulations and obligations and the pitfalls surrounding your signature on any deal from a start-up to buying a business or franchise, you will realize that you need a good lawyer. Although the lawyer may not seem to provide any benefit to the management tripod, you can be sure of one thing. The lawyer is great at preventative maintenance. In other words, prevent the problem before it happens.

You require a lawyer from the outset. A good lawyer will ensure that you conform to the many regulations that exist in the business world. You should think of your lawyer as another confidante and business advisor. However, you should bear in mind that no lawyer can be an authority in all areas of the law. There are lawyers who have particular strengths in franchising, estate planning, tax planning, corporate work, and family problems. Your principal lawyer may not be the expert you need in a specialized case. It is important, therefore, that you know your lawyer's strengths and weaknesses. The onus is on you as the chief financial officer, chief executive officer, and chief operating officer of your business to be certain that your lawyer is skilled in the area for which he or she has been engaged.

Here are some of the specific areas in which a lawyer can be of invaluable assistance to you. As discussed above, a major decision when you start out is whether to incorporate or to operate as a proprietorship. You can discuss the details with your lawyer (as well as your accountant) to determine what is best for you.

If you have decided to take on a partner to strengthen one of your weak areas and also provide some additional capital, then your lawyer is the key player in developing a good partnership agreement. Taking on a partner is just as important as starting the business. Make that preventative-maintenance move and have a proper agreement drawn up by a competent lawyer at the start. Don't procrastinate and put off doing it until you "have time." There are too many examples of small-business partnerships that have problems that cannot be resolved in a reasonable manner because a shareholders' agreement does not exist. This is costly to both parties.

If you have developed a new product that you wish to protect, then your lawyer can help you register the patent in your name. Likewise, if you have developed a design, symbol, or logo that you plan to use for a long time, your lawyer can help you register it as a trademark.

If you happen to be buying a business or a franchise, then a lawyer can prepare the necessary documents and deal with the vendor's lawyer to be certain that your legal position is covered.

No doubt you will be leasing premises for your new venture. Don't ever sign an offer to lease without first having the details reviewed by your lawyer. The small print of a lease—the renewal and subletting provisions and many other items—must be dealt with and resolved before your name is on the line. The lease was drawn up by the lessor's lawyer. You can be sure that it is loaded with phrases in the lessor's favor. You will find it very difficult to have some of these standard phrases changed, but you should at least have your lawyer outline any of the possible problems.

Although it will not be a problem at the outset, employers eventually find that the term "wrongful dismissal" pops up as a tremendous annoyance and cost. Your lawyer can help you deal with this new problem for business owners. In other words, as discussed earlier in this chapter, if you intend to dismiss an employee, failure to take the proper steps can result in litigation, legal fees, and substantial severance-allowance payments.

If you find that you or your company are being sued, then a good lawyer can help settle the action as soon as possible, minimizing legal costs and damages and perhaps settling out of court.

In some cases your lawyer can be of great assistance in collecting some major slow or bad accounts receivable.

Granted, you can file smaller accounts in the small claims court, but the larger amounts require the heavy hand of your lawyer. Like your accountant, your lawyer can be used as a confidante and can bring objectivity to your discussions and to delicate internal matters dealing with the company's business.

How do you find the right lawyer? The best approach is to ask for referrals from your accountant, banker, business associates, and trade association. When you receive the names of two or three lawyers with backgrounds that seem to fit your needs, arrange to visit them in their offices. Observe the staff and surroundings to help you determine whether the "chemistry" is right. Law is a highly technical field and your lawyer's territory is foreign to you. You should have confidence in his or her skills in both legal matters and general business. Your interview should cover the areas you consider important to your business.

Like your accountant, your lawyer usually charges by the hour. You should get an estimate of the time and costs involved in dealing with your lawyer. When you have selected your law firm, you should obtain a written understanding of the services and cost estimates. Once you have chosen your lawyer, remember these five important tips on controlling legal fees:

1. Don't reach for the telephone to call your lawyer every time a potential legal matter arises. First try to settle any items you can using your own business sense. The moment you feel you are over your head, call your lawyer.
2. Don't fight for "principles" that are really matters of pride.
3. Use a less senior or less expensive lawyer for small items (collections) and an old pro for more serious corporate matters such as contracts or litigation.
4. Always try to contact your lawyer during normal business hours and see the lawyer in his or her office to minimize premium charges for travel time.
5. Insist on an itemized statement of charges with each bill. Don't be reluctant to discuss the amount of the bill on receipt.

Advisory Panels

You have now established three key outside advisors: your accountant, banker, and lawyer. Another strong spoke in the success wheel is an advisory panel. This is an informal group that acts as a board of directors, but the advisory panel's members do not have the liabilities associated with being a director of your company. An advisory panel should consist of three to four outsiders who can bring a complement of expertise your meetings. The main advantage that your advisors will have is objectivity. They will have no axe to grind regarding your personnel or regarding any other details of your business. You should determine an advisor's fee for each meeting. This can range from a nice dinner to $500. Three advisors should cover all of the legs of the management tripod: marketing, operations, and finance. The meeting should be structured with an agenda. Each of the advisors should receive a package of financial information and other data pertaining to the meeting together with the agenda a minimum of one week before any meeting. Although it may be considered a quasi-social function, you, the business owner, should keep in mind that this is your money and your future that your advisors are talking about. As a result, the meeting should be kept to a reasonably serious and conscientious level.

Informal Business Consortia

In addition to this, you should consider assembling a group of business owners in the same business, for the purpose of exchanging information, ideas, and discussing common problems. For example, there is a group of dry-cleaning operators located in southern Ontario who describe themselves as the Dry Cleaners Educational Management Group. This group of eight dry-cleaning owners meets monthly to discuss the various aspects of the individual businesses. I might also add that the owners are not competing with each other due to their location. Each of the owners has different weaknesses and strengths. They, in fact, feed on each other's knowledge. They reinforce their meetings with outside specialists from time to time, who can provide input in the areas that they have defined as being general weaknesses.

On one occasion, an owner made a presentation on a major piece of equipment that he was purchasing for his dry-cleaning plant. At that point, he was sold on the purchase. But after a few hours of discussion, pointed questions, and general input from the other seven members, the owner decided not to make the purchase. It became evident that another piece of equipment would do a better job at less cost.

This group has come to realize the importance of financial records and current financial statements. They have established a standard chart of accounts for each company's general ledger and will be receiving monthly financial statements for their own position and a consolidation financial statement for the group. From the current accurate information, each member will then be able to measure where he or she stands in terms of the group.

8

CREATING AND SATISFYING DEMAND

Marketing is a word that has traditionally been misused. The odds are that if you ask ten people what marketing is, nine would suggest that it is selling. Actually, marketing includes all steps or activities necessary to place goods or services in the hands of the consumer. In other words, marketing begins the moment the basic idea for a product or service emerges and continues through to the production, shipping, delivering, warehousing, and distribution of the product, when the item finally comes to rest in the hands of the ultimate user. To differentiate marketing from sales, consider marketing as the method with which you will attack the marketplace and sales as dealing with customers to get the business.

Marketing is the first leg of your management tripod. In other words, you have to "get the business." This means more than just selling. It means that all of the other grass roots and creative work have to be done upfront in order to get the product or service to the marketplace, where it can be sold. In fact, some of the functions of the operations leg (see Chapter 7) overlap into the marketing area since operations deals with personnel and the need to deliver the product or service that was sold. Then, too, the finance leg (Chapters 10 and 11) overlaps into marketing since finance deals with all of the financial areas of the business and the profit goals.

In this chapter, we will discuss a range of marketing concerns: seeking out the markets for the product or service; creating a demand; choosing effective selling techniques; advertising; sales promotion; and questions pertaining to warehousing and distribution; as well as customer service and follow-up.

To start, you, the small-business owner, will need a fully developed marketing plan that is based on understanding your customers' needs, your company's resources, and the nature of the competition. You will also need a sales plan that projects revenues. This plan was discussed in Chapter 6: Planning for the Cash.) Then, you will have to learn to respond to the marketplace as trends in your industry change. Remember that true entrepreneurs are flexible, learn from experience, and know when to ask for help.

The Business Concept

The first step is to define your business concept. In other words, exactly what does your company do? Now, the problem that plagues many definitions of business concepts is narrow vision. A classic example is Central Railway, the major railway company in the United States that went into receivership. That company's owners defined their business concept as operating a railway. Unfortunately that was myopic, particularly because their customers relied on the company first and foremost as a distributor of goods and services. A business concept based on that function would have opened up thinking in the direction of delivery of goods by train, truck, and airplane, and would have prevented the company's demise as a result of the obsolescence of railways.

In defining your own business concept, you should know what your target market wants. Regardless of the product or service, you are really only selling a "benefit." The benefit will take one of three forms: 1. prestige, 2. price, and 3. peace of mind. I will buy the high-priced car for prestige. Or I will buy the low-priced car because of the price. Or I will buy the car with the ultimate in safety features for peace of mind.

You should determine what principal benefits you plan to provide to your customers. In other words, if you have suggested that the business that you are "really in" is a low-volume, high-price, high-gross-profit, full-service retail operation, then this would form part of your definition. For example, if you are in the retail clothing business, your definition of your business concept may read like this: "I am a high-fashion retailer handling upper-end lines of quality products on an exclusive basis at a reasonable (not a discount) price. I will provide good customer service." One of the key points in the book *In Search of Excellence* was "staying close to the customer." Providing customer service and knowing what the customer wants should form part of your thinking in defining your business concept.

Customers are your greatest asset. The secret is to get new customers and keep them. So, how do you go about getting the customers? The first step is to establish an image for your company that creates a demand for your product or services. The image is developed through personal contact, promotional material, advertising, and public relations.

It is important for you to look at your business through your customers' eyes. What benefits do you offer your customers? Prestige? Price? Or peace of mind? Also, what are the needs of your targeted customers? What problems might they have that could be resolved with the help of your product or service? If you can define what your target customers need or want, then you can deliver a current product or maybe modify your product to satisfy this need.

Because new trends always seem to be emerging, it is important to keep up to date in your industry and constantly to consider how such trends might affect or relate to your own products or services.

Once you have created some demand, then the next step is to sell your product or service to potential customers.

Creating Demand: Advertising, Promotion, and Public Relations

In order to sell your product or service, you need to create a demand. This demand can be created through advertising, promotion, and public relations.

Although these terms are often considered virtually synonymous and are indeed closely related, in fact each one refers to a distinct area of activity. Strictly speaking, advertising refers to the effective description of products, services, and prices in print or electronic media; promotion refers to the effective strategies and means employed to communicate a company's image and benefits to its target market; and public relations refers to the development and maintenance of positive contact pertaining to business with the public.

For many new small-business owners, the cost of advertising is prohibitive. Advertising can take the form of a television commercial, a radio commercial, or an advertisement in a national or local newspaper. The major problem with this type of advertising is that you are directing it to the masses as opposed to specifically targeted markets. In other words, this is more like a shotgun approach than a rifle shot.

As a small-business owner, you probably do not have the financing to use the shotgun approach. You would be better advised to use the rifle-shot approach and look to other media or types of activity to create the demand for your product or service. For example, if you are in the high-fashion clothing business, a very select group will be potential customers. It makes no sense to advertise where only a small percentage of the readership or viewers will be potential customers for your store. A better alternative for this high-fashion retailer will be to obtain a mailing list of senior executives in the area and develop a direct-mail marketing campaign.

On the other hand, the example of Alex Tilley's nationwide advertisements to develop his mail-order program for the Tilley Endurables hat has proven to be extremely successful in describing not only the Tilley hat, but the other clothing products to the masses. Each product or service will be different, and you must develop your own advertising plan based on your market analyses and the target market.

If you are selling a product or service to a specific industry, it may make sense to place ads in the trade magazines.

To promote your product or service, you can consider a few alternatives. First, of course, is the traditional brochure describing the details of your product or service. In addition, your stationery, cards, letterheads, and so forth should be developed to provide the kind of image that you wish to convey to your target market. In many cases, a descriptive logo is important. Recognition of your company and products will assist greatly in opening doors for you and your sales staff. It may be appropriate to utilize the specialty advertising industry to develop a practical "handout" with the name of the company, logo, or product described. For a high-priced product, this handout should be more expensive and somewhat sophisticated to provide the correct image for your activity. On the other hand, if you are selling to the mass market, you cannot afford a high-priced item and maybe a simple ballpoint pen or calendar may be appropriate.

Public relations is sometimes the best and least expensive approach to creating the demand for your product or service. Public relations can consist of articles in trade magazines, speaking engagements to local community clubs, TV or radio interviews on subjects related to your product or service, and articles published in either trade or general publications that will reach your market. Prior to commencing my business, I found it very difficult to speak in public, had no skills for writing articles, and TV interviews would be considered sheer terror. Well, I realized that this must change if I was to develop my financial-services practice. In 1973 I was asked to speak at a small-business conference at Ryerson Polytechnical Institute in Toronto. The preparation time was considerable for my fifteen-minute talk, and the anxiety was almost overwhelming. By 1980, I was writing a biweekly column in the *Financial Times of Canada* and had developed and was teaching a credit course in the MBA program at York University in Toronto. I am currently very active in presenting financial-management seminars and writing monthly columns for national magazines.

Depending on your product or service, it may be appropriate to sponsor a little-league baseball team, hockey team, or any activity where you will be considered a "good guy." This is one way of making your product or service more acceptable and more recognized in the eyes of potential customers. When you develop a mailing list of your target market, you may wish to consider a bimonthly or quarterly newsletter or some method of communication by direct mail to keep your name in front of this target market. It is also important to become involved in social and sports-club activities. The prime purpose of this is not to obtain business, but to develop contacts and associations both with your market and with other business people. The continual development of your network is necessary to the long-term success of your company. This is a good approach.

The use of press releases sent to the local media can be a good form of free publicity. These press releases may consist of items regarding the product, a sale to a major customer, the introduction of a new or senior employee, a description of activities with your little-league baseball or hockey team, or anything that can be of interest to the local media for publication where the name of your product or company will be included.

If marketing is not your background and you do not feel comfortable handling the advertising, promotion, and public relations directly, then you should engage the services of a small-business advertising agency. This may sound scary and expensive, but it doesn't have to be. One approach is to ask your network which companies might be suitable for your business. You should then interview two or three of the principals and ask for a proposal. A proposal should be the result of conversations with you about your product or services and the target market you wish to reach. The proposal should include, in broad terms, the approach to be used by the advertising agency together with estimated costs for their fees and out-of-pocket expenses for graphics, media, and printing costs.

In the initial stages of a start-up, this may seem like an unwarranted cost. In fact, deciding whether or not to engage an advertising agency is part of your decision-making process. This decision is also part of starting your business off on the right foot. In many cases, part of the start-up costs should include the necessary fees and expenses of establishing your program to "create demand."

Sales

The ultimate goal of marketing is to get sales. A sales plan targets the amount of sales you want to achieve. This was discussed in Chapter 6 when you prepared your business plan. What you developed was a formal sales plan where you had detailed sales by customers by months for the first year. In the initial stages you may be the only salesperson. But regardless of how many salespeople join your company in the future, you, the small-business owner, must be closely involved with sales. If your job at the big company was in operations or finance and this isn't your bag, then you had better take some courses, read some books, or hire consultants who counsel you in dealing in this area. In virtually every small business, the owner is the chief source of sales.

Selling Techniques

Here are some tips for the nonsales-oriented entrepreneur on how you might handle some of your prospective customers and possibly "close" a deal. It is important to make a good first impression. A bad first impression can mean a customer lost forever. The key is to respect your customer's time and be prompt at any appointments. Be a good listener and know when to shut up.

If a customer has a special request, do whatever you can to customize your product or services to comply. However, be careful that every customer doesn't give you a special request and you end up changing your whole product line at great expense. But if an occasion arises when you can accommodate a customer, you will impress him or her and this could possibly lead to other sales.

The two major problems in making a sale are the indecisive customer and the one who puts up objections to your sales pitch. The indecisive customer is really looking for reassurance that your product or service is the right thing for him or her. The secret here is to ask questions to determine the customer's real needs. Then offer two or, at the most, three recommendations and the merits of each. Sometimes the customer will consider this great assistance and will feel comfortable and confident in buying one of the recommendations.

The customer who is throwing up objections is at least listening to what you have to say and showing some interest. This is where your product knowledge and knowing the customer's needs will pay off. If you have a tangible product, then by all means let the customer try it on, taste it, drive it, or whatever, and then deal with any comments or objections as they are presented.

Some years ago, a friend of mine who is a salesman told me of an experience that he had at a recent sales meeting with his big company. Due to car trouble, he was late for the meeting of about ten salespeople and as he walked in the door, he heard the presenter yelling, "Shut up." My friend was quite shocked to hear such an outburst which was evidently chastising one or more of the audience. But that was not the case; rather, the presenter was demonstrating to the sales team how to get an order. His point was that there is a time to talk, a time to listen, and a time to close. He indicated that too many so-called salespeople talk themselves in and out of a sale. The message is clear: once you have determined that your customer is ready to buy, stop talking.

Customers are likely to display two types of buying signals: verbal and nonverbal. The buying signals will vary from talking positively about the product to making calculations, nodding, or reaching for the sales contract. This is something that you will have to learn. But when you recognize it, ask for the order. There is a statistic that indicates that almost two-thirds of all sales calls conclude without the salesperson asking for an order.

If you get a no, then it is a good idea to follow up from time to time by mail or telephone. In other words, remember the old expression: If at first you don't succeed, try, try again. Mind you, there is a point when you stop trying and wasting your time.

Once you have closed the sale, then the next step is to do everything to make the customer feel that you have exceeded their expectations in the product or service that they purchased. There is another statistic that suggests that you will hear from four percent of the dissatisfied customers. However, a silent ninety-six percent of dissatisfied customers will simply never come back. But that's just the tip of the iceberg: not only will they never come back, but they will tell other people who may have been prospective clients or customers for your new venture. The loss of one customer in the early months of your start-up will have a long-term negative effect on the growth of your business.

Customer Service and Sales Staff

Customers who feel that they have received more than they paid for will be very quick to recommend your company. A happy customer will refer future customers. Future happy customers will refer additional customers. In time, the initial happy customer may prove to have been the source of your future expansion. The golden rule applies to the manner in which you deal with your customers. "Do unto others as you would have them do unto you."

In other words, put yourself in your customer's position and make a list of the items that you would wish to see happen in order for you to be completely happy with the product or service. If you are providing an ongoing service or products to your clients, then you will, no doubt, be making regular calls or visits to maintain continuity with your customers. However, as you grow, it is important to establish a customer service program that will provide each of your customers with an ongoing relationship and a follow-up to the individual deliveries and quality of the product. Although much of this will be dealt with by staff, you must maintain as close a relationship as possible to each of your customers or clients. Customer service starts at the top and in many cases, your good long-term customers really like to deal with the "boss." Although you may not be carrying out some of the detailed functions to support these customers or clients, they do not want to feel forgotten by the first person whom they met when they became customers of your business.

However, you will not be able to maintain as close contact with them as you might wish as your company grows. It is, therefore, important to hire salespeople who can carry on in the tradition that you started. This means that you must hire salespeople who can maintain the same customer follow-up and who can make a customer feel like he or she is a "somebody." In Chapter 7, we discussed how to go about hiring staff. You must prioritize the characteristics that you want in the salespeople whom you wish to hire. There is no such thing as a precise profile of the perfect salesperson. The sales staff in a retail operation, where the customers approach them for service, are much different from the sales staff who must hustle up business, knock on doors, and be strong closers. In each of these two categories, there are many profiles. For example, in a retail operation, the salesperson does not have to be a strong self-starter, but he or she must know how to handle the clientele. The clientele will vary, of course, depending on the industry. For example, a salesperson in a high-fashion clothing store must have the appearance to suit the position, as well as the manner to deal with clients who will be paying $1,000 plus for custom-made suits and the necessary accessories. The salesperson in a super-discount, warehouse-retail operation, on the other hand, will be an altogether different type of person. The secret in this type of operation is to let the client think that he or she is getting a deal; consequently, the salesperson should adopt a less sophisticated approach to avoid intimidating potential customers.

Whether your business is retail or selling direct, the personality of the sales staff must be compatible with the product. A highly technical product requires a highly technical person, as he or she will be dealing with highly technical people in the client company who are responsible for signing the order.

But your sales staff will also need certain qualifications that are common to all salespeople. First and foremost, they must know the product or service. You must make certain that every sales rep knows in detail the merits of your product or service and is able to answer the various questions that can be asked of them during a sales presentation.

The next important qualification is sincerity. The salesperson's story must be believable, and customers must feel that he or she has a true interest in their well-being. The next qualification is "hard work." The outside salesperson must work very diligently to set up the various appointments, demonstrations, and close the deal. For retail salespeople, this is not a necessity. For the most part, the customers come to them. The other qualification can be summarized in one word: personality. The type of personality varies with the type of product for sale. This must be established before you hire any salespeople.

Now that you have set your priorities and hired what you consider to be the correct sales staff, you should realize that over sixty percent will probably fail as salespeople in your company in the first year. The predominant reason for failure is a lack of hard work on the part of the new salesperson. This failure can be the result of the individual's personal priorities or the result of being placed in a sales position that is not compatible with his or her personality. Another major reason is that these salespeople get discouraged if they do not progress substantially in the early months. If your product is high priced and requires considerable lead time before closing a deal, then you may have to take necessary steps to provide encouragement to your salespeople during this time. However, if you are selling a consumable product that is short term, then you may have to take more time to train and supervise the salespeople whom you hire in the initial months. Remember that you have spent a lot of time and money upfront to hire these people and to provide some initial training. It bears repeating. If you hire the wrong salesperson who ends up turning off some of your prospective customers or even some of your current customers, then you will not only lose the customer and potential sale, but you will lose numerous sales in the future that would have been the result of referrals by these people. Surveys conducted with retail automotive dealers indicated that hiring the wrong salesperson could result in reduced future profits of over $100,000 per sales rep.

Strange as it might seem, another reason for lost salespeople is that they fail to follow the instructions provided during the training program. Some of your self-starting salespeople will be independent and will be trying some of their own ways to sell your product. Again, this comes down to the priorities that you establish when you hire salespeople. A self-starter will be independent, harder to handle, and require closer supervision to make sure he or she is adhering to the tried-and-proven methods of selling your product. If you find that there is a regular turnover of your sales staff, then you had better get your act together, review your priorities, hire, train, and supervise the right people to sell your product.

An initial investment in the training of your sales staff is critical. Without sales, you have no business. Everything starts with selling. In many cases, the salesperson is the only personal link to the customer. This person represents your company and must be carefully trained about the many facets of your product. As suggested above, the key item to be a successful salesperson is knowledge of the product, and this comes from good training from you.

In the initial stages of your company, however, you cannot afford to hire a person to be trained as a sales representative. You must hire proven salespeople to sell your product. The inherent sales skills must be in place as you will not have the time or probably the inclination to take a raw recruit and perform the grass-roots training. Your training should consist of product knowledge, knowledge of your company, details of prospective buyers, and how the proven sales techniques already learned can be applied to your particular product. When you are advertising for sales help, then, be certain to put "experienced" in front of your description. Experienced in your industry, of course, is the ultimate.

If your product or service requires written proposals to finalize any sale, then you had better make sure that any salesperson you hire has the writing skills to complete these proposals. As you are no doubt aware, we have major problems in Canada with university graduates who can't write and high school graduates who can't add. If you are going to hire a hot-shot salesman who can't add or put words together to form a reasonable sentence, then you can be sure of one thing—this person will not be able to prepare a reasonable proposal to sell your products or services.

9

OPERATIONAL CONTROLS

Another important ingredient for the success of any business is establishing proper operational controls. As a small-business owner, you will be required to make numerous decisions on a daily basis. Every time a small-business owner makes a decision, it is possible to make a mistake. It follows, therefore, that if he or she can minimize the number of decisions to be made, that this will minimize the number of mistakes. Operational controls are one way of minimizing the number of decisions to be made. Key areas where controls should be established at the outset include purchases and payments, sales and cash receipts, and inventory and cash. Many other controls are necessary, but these are the main areas.

Studies indicate that a large percentage of all business problems can be traced to inadequate or nonexisting operational controls. Controls are systems or procedures established to safeguard the company's assets and to optimize profitability. Adequate controls effectively reduce the amount of time the owner needs to spend scrutinizing business activities and minimize the number of decisions to be made.

With good operational controls, a business owner can be reasonably assured that:

• for all purchase invoices paid, goods were received and the correct price paid;

- inventory purchased is either on hand or sold and billed;
- all products shipped to customers were billed and the accounts collected.

Simple operational control systems can be established for the one-person show and be carried on through the company as it expands and takes on additional personnel. Don't make the mistake of suggesting you know what is going on because you are there all the time. These basic operational control systems, set up for the one-person show, can be used as the company grows and takes on new personnel who will not have the same attitude or interest as you, the owner.

Accounts Payable Systems

Regardless of the size of your business, a purchase order must be used for all purchases. This can be a three-part standard form purchased at the local office supply company. The first copy is sent to the supplier, the second is used as a receiving report, and the third is for expedition in the office. The purchase order should record the description, quantity, and price of the items ordered. On receipt of the goods, the receiver records the quantity received and checks it with the receiving report (copy two), and signs the receiving copy. The receiving report is then sent to the office where it will be matched with the forthcoming supplier's invoice. All details should be checked, and the supplier's invoice approved for payment. If there are any discrepancies, suppliers should be notified immediately and a credit note requested. When the cheque is prepared, it is important that you sign each cheque and review all invoices attached to be certain that you are only paying for the invoices that are approved. After signing, a large "paid" stamp must be placed on each supplier's invoice to eliminate any duplicate payments. (It should be noted here that supplier's statements, as opposed to invoices, should not be paid but should only be used for reconciling the amounts owing to the supplier. In my view, they should be thrown out immediately.)

I suggest that an open-file system be used in preference to accounts payable subledgers. An alphabetic accordion file can be used to hold the unpaid, but approved, accounts payable. A listing should be made at the end of each month in what is referred to as an accounts payable trial balance, aged by the month the purchase was incurred. This listing itemizes the individual supplier on the left side. Across the top are columns showing the total amount owed to the supplier, the current or dollar amount purchased in the current month, and in 30 days, 60 days, and over-90 days. This gives you a bird's-eye view of how you are handling your suppliers and which overdue accounts may cause you some problems in the future.

Using purchase orders when you start your small business may seem redundant, but let me assure you that without them, you will pay for goods that are not received and you will pay for goods twice. The only change to the above procedure is that it may not be necessary to send the first copy to the supplier.

Accounts Receivable Systems

In a wholesale and manufacturing company, a sales-order system must be used for all sales. A multi-part sales-order form is best for all incoming orders. Three copies are sent to the warehouse or plant to instruct the personnel to ship the necessary product. On completion of the shipment, one of the three copies is returned to the office indicating the individual items that have been shipped. It is mandatory that nothing be shipped from the warehouse or the plant without this sales order.

The office will then take the original copies of the sales order (which are serially pre-numbered for control purposes), complete the quantity shipped, extend the unit prices, add the extensions for the total invoice amount, and add any taxes or shipping costs. This procedure must be completed no later than the day following the shipment, and the invoice must be mailed to the customer at that time.

Again, this might seem redundant in a very small operation. Well, you can be sure of one thing. If you don't use this type of system, you will ship goods that will not be billed or collected. This procedure will virtually guarantee that all items shipped are billed, provided the system is adhered to.

Again, an open-file system is common in small businesses.

A copy of the sales invoice can be filed in an alphabetic accordion file and then matched up with payments as they are received. At month-end, a listing of the unpaid invoices should be made. The list should have the customer's name on the left side with columns across the top that read Total (the total amount owed to you by the customer) and Current, 30 Days, 60 Days, and over-90 Days, referring to the time when the products were shipped and billed to the customers. This is referred to as an accounts receivable trial balance.

Inventory Control

Another control system that should be implemented for retailers, wholesalers, and manufacturers is inventory control. This must be established to make sure that reasonable quantities of the correct products are being purchased. Incorrect purchasing can result in an over-inventory of certain products and an inadequate inventory of others. This system can be a simple card system of the key products which will indicate the inventory units on hand at any given time, the record of purchases outstanding, quantities received, and quantities shipped. A reasonable level of minimum and maximum quantities can be established for each of these key products and the purchasing performed accordingly. By the way, this can be handled by your personal computer, which will be discussed in Chapter 12.

In addition, it is important that physical control be maintained to safeguard these assets. Physical controls will be used to safeguard outside and inside theft. Very strict security should be maintained for high value, easily marketable items.

Cash Control

In retail operations, cash control should be implemented to be certain that all of the sales are recorded in the cash register or on the sales slip, and the cash is accounted for on a daily basis. For a little over $1,000, cash registers can be purchased that will provide you with an analysis of sales by product groups together with other details on cash, Visa, MasterCard, and so forth. There are two keys to these registers. The Y key is used by the individual cashiers to balance their funds when they come off duty. The Z key is your control key, and it accumulates the totals of the activity in the cash register so that you can confirm the balances indicated on the cashiers' reports.

The major problem with retailers is not necessarily the balancing of the cash. The major problem is "under rings." If the cashier under rings the purchases, the cash will balance but the inventory won't. There is the example of a retailer who wished to sell his store. We were approached to provide consulting services on the sale and prepare the financial details for any prospective purchaser. The information provided by the owner indicated that the gross profit in the store was 35%. On reviewing the financial statements, I noticed that the gross profit percent on the financial statements signed by the chartered accountant was 27%. With sales of about $800,000, this amounted to a shortfall of $64,000 in gross profit. In discussions with the owner, I was informed that for two years, one of the clerks had been under ringing sales, which probably accounted for the shortfall. Believe it or not, that's about $128,000 of lost income.

This retailer received statements once a year, about six months after the year-end, and it wasn't until the third year that the company realized that there was a major problem with its gross profit. The retailer observed that when one particular cashier had the day off, customers would arrive, ask for her and when they were told she wasn't there, they would comment, "I'll come back tomorrow." They have no proof of what was happening except that when the cashier was laid off, the gross profit mysteriously increased to about the 34% level.

In Chapter 12, where we discuss computers, we will deal with the advantages of implementing a point of sale computer for retail operations. This will virtually eliminate the under-ring problem.

10

THE FINANCE LEG

The third leg of the management tripod is the finance leg. There is no point "getting the business" and "doing the business" if you are not going to make a reasonable profit. Although small business has achieved an impressive statistical profile in start-ups and job creation, it has also spearheaded one very sad statistic: 80% of small businesses can be expected to fail within the first three to five years of operation.

Failure can include anything from total financial failure or receivership to mergers or the retirement of an owner who sells off the assets of the business or simply does not bother to ensure its continuance. The odds are that many of the owners of such small businesses have lost all or substantially all of their personal wealth. If you were to believe everything you read in the newspapers, you might think that the glut of small-business failures is caused by recessions, high-interest rates, mail strikes, the government, and in general, a poor economy. But how would you explain the failure of companies when low-interest rates prevail, when there have been no postal strikes, and when the economy is thriving? And why can some companies remain competitive in a poor economic climate? Believe it or not, in difficult times, some firms do better. In short, winners thrive and losers flounder. Another category of small businesses, often referred to as "the living dead," can generally survive in a good economic climate, but cannot withstand inflation, high-interest rates, and overall downturns in the economy.

Who are the failures? In my view, they are individuals who have not earned the title of entrepreneur. And what is involved in earning that title? The answer is simple: getting control. In other words a person *in effective control* of a commercial undertaking is a true entrepreneur and, in my view, can survive most of the negative market and financial conditions that are an inherent part of the business world.

The obvious question is: "How do I get control?" Believe it or not, it is very simple: Be a good manager. Although the term *entrepreneurship* suggests that you should be a tremendous innovator, I maintain that it is equally, if not more, important for entrepreneurs to be skilled managers in complete control of their chosen ventures.

Fundamentals of Financial Management

Good management means making sound (and consistent) decisions. And making sound decisions is a three-step process: 1. gather the facts; 2. measure the facts; and 3. interpret the facts.

The first basic step to planning is to assemble information. This information consists of facts surrounding any given circumstance. Similarly, the first step to making basic decisions is to assemble the facts or gather the facts, and base decisions on facts as opposed to hearsay or general industry yardsticks that could very well be outdated. The secret is to *gather pertinent facts* on a daily, weekly, and monthly basis. In business, a bare minimum in fact-gathering is the monthly financial statement that charts your progress in the key categories of the business plan that you developed to start off your business. *Measuring the facts* means calculating key ratios for the balance sheet and profit-and-loss statement. Decisions can be made only after these measurements of the facts—the key ratios— have been *interpreted* through a comparison with pre-determined thresholds or industry statistics. Obviously, if the ratios indicate that you are not on track according to your business plan or that you are falling short of industry standards, then you have succeeded in defining a problem. And once the problem is defined, you are 90% of the way to resolving it.

Gathering Financial Facts: The Monthly Financial Report

You can be sure of one thing: if you don't have accurate current information, based at *minimum* on monthly financial statements, you will be treading the primrose path to failure.

Several years ago, a chartered bank asked our firm to review the financial situation of one of its customers. Until two or three years before, the company in question had not needed to use the bank's line of credit. Its land, buildings, and equipment had all been paid for and the company appeared to be financially secure. But in the last two years, the company's annual losses (without accounting for the owner's salary) were in the area of $150,000. The owner of this small business had been in the habit of receiving financial statements six months after the year-end, and was therefore unaware that, during the second year, he had sustained the losses that he had recognized in the first year. Consequently, in the seventh month of the third year, the company had sustained losses in the two and one-half years of about $400,000. By the way, he was now using about $400,000 of his line of credit. On reviewing the previous year's financial statements, we were quick to realize that the sales of about $700,000 rendered a gross loss after all manufacturing expenses of about $20,000. The other $130,000 was for selling and general administrative expenses. To turn this around, two simple things were done. First, monthly financial statements were implemented immediately. And second, a simple cost system was estalished similar to that discussed in Chapter 11. At the end of the third year, the hemorrhaging had been curtailed, and the loss was $110,000. In the fourth year, the net profit before management salaries was $35,000. At the end of the fifth year, this was increased to over $150,000. This current accurate information made it clear to the small-business owner that he had too much staff and that he was not pricing his products for profitable sales. The combination of the simple cost system and the monthly financial statements (which were compared to a turnaround plan) allowed the owner to make the informed decisions necessary to return the company to a good, profitable position. I might also add that if this had not taken place, then the bank would no doubt have called the loan, and it is questionable whether the company's assets would have been able to cover the bank loan position and the receiver's fees. The natural backstop for the bank, of course, is the small-business owner's home.

Why don't all small-business owners have monthly financial reports? The most common reasons given are that "they are too time-consuming and costly" and "not necessary." Well, this is nonsense. A system that is properly set up is not time-consuming and will not be costly. First of all, you must have someone recording basic transactions in your book of accounts. I must say that, in most cases, small business owners feel the necessity for this. The only thing stopping them from taking this information and preparing a financial statement is a little know-how. The odds are that the bookkeeper can provide this financial information by summarizing the details each month-end. It might take another hour or two. An alternative to this, of course, is to use an outside computer service or, in many cases, your outside accountant can prepare these on his or her in-house computer bookkeeping system. The costs for outside services can be upward from $100 per month to, say, $250 to $300 for larger firms. This is obviously not costly, and the detailed records must be prepared anyway. Another alternative is to utilize the personal computer that you, no doubt, have in place in your small business. We will be discussing the use of computers in Chapter 12.

In my view, the main reason that many small-business owners feel that monthly financial reports are unnecessary is the lack of pressure from their bankers and their outside accountants. It never ceases to amaze me that outside accountants don't emphasize the need for this information to their small-business clients. I further do not understand why so many bankers (not all) don't insist upon receiving monthly financial statements when loaning substantial amounts to small-business owners. The reason for receiving the statements is not to review them, but just to make sure that their customers are getting the information with which to manage their businesses properly. Unfortunately, there are still many "second-wave" bankers and outside accountants servicing small-business owners, and they are not aware of this necessary management tool.

Here is an example of the indifference of bankers and accountants. A small-business owner whom I know bought his job. At the time of the purchase, the banker insisted on receiving monthly financial reports to enable him to monitor the progress of the company against the business plan that had been presented. The outside accountant agreed (for a fee) to prepare these monthly financial statements. Three years after the purchase, the banker indicated that he no longer required these monthly financial reports as the majority of the loan had been repaid and he felt comfortable with the management ability of his customer. At this point, his outside accountant ceased preparing the reports as it was not something that he normally did.

Another example of the indifference of accountants is illustrated by a chartered bank that saw the necessity of having financial statements from its customers. The bank's concern was how this could be facilitated without being a major burden on its customers. It was suggested that we would cooperate for a period of six months during which time our company would pay for the set-up and the bank would pay our company an ongoing fee of $150 per month for up to ten of their customers. Senior people in the bank spent considerable time developing a program and communicating this through one of their commercial branches. I went personally with the respective account manager to visit various clients in order to review this project and sign them up for a no-cost six-month trial basis. After six months, they could continue by paying $150 per month or discontinue the project.

Well, you can believe it or not, but not one of the bank's customers that we visited agreed to the project. In every case, they had to talk to their accountant and the normal answer was, this is "unnecessary."

One of the classic negative responses was: "If we find out that we are losing money, we will only worry." A word to the wise: "Don't be an ostrich."

A typical example of the type of information you should

be receiving on a monthly basis is: 1. a balance sheet; 2. a profit-and-loss statement, indicating sales, cost of sales, gross profit, wages, occupancy and other expenses, and net profit before income taxes; 3. subschedules, setting out by product groups, sales, cost of sales, and inventory; 4. subschedules setting out breakdowns of wages and benefits, occupancy (rent, repairs, property taxes, utilities), and all other expenses for selling and administration.

The monthly financial information should be set up in a format that will provide you with the key information to make good decisions.

Measuring the Facts: Key Ratios

The next step is to measure the results indicated on the monthly financial statements. The individual numbers on the statements can mean very little without calculating some of the key ratios or measurements. For example, a friend of mine was dealing with another accounting firm and wanted me to review his financial statements. His question was: "What do you think?" My question back to him was: "What do you think?" His reaction was: "I guess I am making X dollars per year." My next question was: "Is that what it should be?" The answer: "I don't know." My friend's company was earning in excess of $200,000 per year after payments to him, and he did not understand the financial statements.

When you buy yourself a job and become your own boss, you are the chief financial officer. You cannot abdicate from this role. It's your money, and you better be aware of the financial implications. And don't say: "That's for bean counters." The best way to understand the numbers is to calculate some of the key ratios. If you happen to take a big-business course in one of the business schools in Canada, you might find there are hundreds of possible ratios that can be used. I like to suggest the following simple ratios are all that you require in order to monitor the affairs of your business:

1. *Current ratio:* This is calculated by dividing the current assets by the current liabilities. It indicates your ability to service your current obligations. The higher the ratio,

the greater the cushion. The bank is very uneasy if this ratio is under 1.5. (See Exhibit 14.) In this instance, the current ratio is C/E or $160/$130 = 1.2

2. *Debt-to-equity ratio:* This is calculated by dividing the total liabilities by the shareholder's equity. This expresses the relationship between the amounts put up to finance your business by the creditors (including the bank) and by you. The higher the ratio, the greater the risk assumed by your creditors. At present, bankers are very cautious about dealing with companies whose debt-to-equity ratio is in excess of 3.0. In Exhibit 14, the debt-to-equity ratio is F/G or $150/$40 = 3.75. We suggested earlier that when you invest your own money in the company, it should be in the form of a note from the shareholder. This amount should be included in the shareholder's equity and not included in liabilities.

3. *Accounts receivable turnover:* This is calculated by dividing the total annual sales by the net accounts receivable. In the case of monthly or interim financial statements, the sales should be annualized (sales of 1 month multiplied by 12, or sales of 5 months multiplied by 12, divided by 5). This ratio measures your ability to manage your accounts receivable collections. The higher the ratio, the better. In Exhibit 14, the accounts receivable turnover is J/A or $600/$75 = 8. If you wish to convert this to the number of days outstanding, divide the actual ratio into 365 days. In this example the ratio is 8, so the number of days unpaid is 46 (365 divided by 8).

4. *Gross profit return on inventory (GPROI):* This is calculated by dividing the annual gross profit by the inventory balance times 100%. If the calculation is made for part of a year, then the gross profit should be annualized in the same manner set out in section three above. This measures your ability to manage the inventory and get the best return on your investment. Many use inventory turnover ratios (annual cost of goods sold divided by inventory balance). This ratio can be misleading. Comparing inventory turnovers for products of different gross profit percents is like comparing apples and oranges. The GPROI, however, combines turnover plus gross profit percentage and

the resulting percentage is a common denominator for all products regardless of the gross profit percentage of the industry. A target percent is 300%. In Exhibit 14, the GPROI is K/B × 100 or $200/$80 × 100 = 250%.

5. *Return on assets:* This is calculated by dividing the annual net profit before income taxes by the total assets times 100. The higher the percentage, the better. This is the ultimate measurement of your management ability. A reasonable yardstick is 30%. In Exhibit 14, the return on assets is Q/D or $10/$190 × 100 = 5%.

EXHIBIT 14

BALANCE SHEET
($000's omitted)

Assets

Current Assets		
Accounts receivable	$ 75	A
Inventory	80	B
Prepaid expenses	5	
Total current assets	160	C
Fixtures and Equipment	30	
	$190	D

Liabilities and Shareholders' Equity

Current Liabilities		
Due to bank	$ 40	
Accounts payable	60	
Notes payable within one year	20	Z
Accrued expenses	10	
Total current liabilities	130	E
Notes Payable	20	
Total liabilities	150	F
Shareholders' Equity	40	G
	$190	

NEWCO INC.
INCOME STATEMENT
($000's omitted)

			% of
Sales	$600	J	
Cost of Sales	400		
Gross Profit	200	K	% of Gross Profit
Expenses			
Wages	120	L	60%
Occupancy	25	M	13%
Other	45	N	22%
Total expenses	190	P	95%
Net Profit Before Income Taxes	$ 10	Q	5%

6. *Return on investment:* This is calculated by dividing the annual net profit before income taxes by the shareholder's equity times 100. This expresses the rate of return on your investment in your business and is another indicator of management performance. In Exhibit 14, the return on investment is Q/G or $10/$40 × 100 = 25%. One problem with this ratio is that companies starting out with a lower equity base may be misled by a higher percentage than a more mature company that has built up equity over the years. The true measurement of your management ability is your return on assets.

The above ratios deal with the facts on the balance sheet. They measure the liquidity of your company and your ability to manage the assets. Let's look at the income statement to measure your ability to manage profitability.

7. *Gross profit percentage:* This is calculated by dividing the gross profit by the sales times 100. This measures the gross profit you are receiving from each dollar of sales. The higher the percentage, the better. If you find that this

ratio is reducing over the months, then this will trigger a red flag that will require your immediate attention. It can mean a change in the mix in sales to less profitable items or inefficiency in the plant (in the case of a manufacturing company) or increases in suppliers' prices that have not been reflected in increased selling prices or poor controls. In Exhibit 14, the gross profit percentage is K/J or $200/$600 $\times$ 100 = 33%.

8. *Expense percentage of gross profit:* A traditional method of monitoring expenses is to express them as a percentage of sales. This too can be misleading. Like the inventory turnover, this does not take into account profitability. Therefore, I suggest that all expense percentages be calculated on the gross profit.

   The two major single categories of expenses are wages (including benefits) and occupancy costs. In calculating these percentages of gross profit, I suggest you group wages and benefits as one category and occupancy (including rent, utilities, property taxes, and maintenance) and all other expenses as another. If you happen to purchase your facilities, then the depreciation and interest on the mortgage would replace rent.

   By dividing these costs by the gross profit times 100, you can determine the percentage of these to the gross profit. If you have no industry statistics, then a general yardstick is that wages should be no more than 50%, occupancy 10%, and other expenses 20%. In other words, the net profit before income taxes should be targeted at 20% of the gross profit.

   In Exhibit 14, wages L/K or $120/$200 $\times$ 100 = 60%; occupancy M/K or $25/$200 $\times$ 100 = 12.5%; other N/K or $45/$200 $\times$ 100 = 22.5%.

Interpreting the Facts: Comparisons

The third step in good management and good decision-making is to interpret the results. These key ratios must be compared to your yardsticks or the norms for your industry. This comparison is similar to a doctor taking your temperature. If the doctor does not know what normal is, taking your temperature is pointless.

Exhibit 15 sets out some general yardsticks that can be used by virtually any industry where there are no specific industry statistics. Let's compare Newco Inc. to these yardsticks. Normally, the bank likes a 2.0 current ratio, as this ensures liquidity in the business and the ability for the small business to pay its current obligations, but 1.5 is acceptable. Newco, however, is 1.2 which means that it is very close to not being able to meet its current obligations. This can be corrected by converting some of the short-term debt to long-term or possibly earning more profits and paying down the bank loan. The reduction of current liabilities from $130,000 to, say, $105,000 would bring the current ratio into about a 1.5 position.

EXHIBIT 15

NEWCO INC.
YARDSTICKS

	Minimum Yardsticks	Newco Wholesale Inc.
Current Ratio	1.5	1.2
Debt to Equity	2.0	3.7
GPROI	300%	250%
Return on Assets	20%	5%
Operating — % of Gross Profit	Maximum	
Wages and Benefits	50%	60%
Occupancy	10%	13%
Other	20%	22%
Net Profit	20%	5%

The debt-to-equity ratio of 3.7 is much higher than the yardstick and indicates that the company is over-levered. In the initial stages of any new business, this is common. Normally, the bank is not concerned as they have outside security supporting the bank position. However, if you wish at some future date to get your personal signature off the bank loan, then you will have to manage your balance sheet so that the debt-to-equity ratio is no more than 1.0. In other words, the total liabilities will be no more than the shareholder's equity.

The GPROI is 250% which is reasonably close to the target 300%. The decisions you should consider in order to bring this into line are to: reduce the inventory to, say, $65,000 from $80,000; review the pricing of your products in an effort to increase the overall gross profit to 40%; or increase sales to, say, about $720,000 per year and maintain the same inventory balance.

Return on assets at 5% is far below the minimum target of 20%. This indicates that the net profit before income taxes is far below the norm and efforts should be made to decrease the assets (accounts receivable, inventory, fixed assets) or increase the net profit. As we will discuss below, the net profit is much lower than the target profit as a percentage of gross profit.

All of the operating expenses as a percent of gross profit are high. This is normal in a new company, but planning should take place at the outset to bring these operating ratios into line. Wages are about $20,000 too high. This is probably one person or two part-time people. If the action is taken to bring the GPROI into line and the gross profit to $240,000, then the wages will fall into line at 50% of gross profit. In fact, the resulting net profit will be $50,000 or about 21% of the gross profit.

By getting a monthly financial statement and calculating the key ratios and comparing them to your yardsticks, you have the tools virtually to create profits. By knowing exactly what these should be to meet your business goals, you can make things happen. Without this information, you drift and when things go wrong, you will probably blame the government or the economy. Gathering the facts, measuring the facts, interpreting the facts, and using them is the lifeblood of your business and future success.

As a by-product, you will be familiar with the details of the operation of your business and will be able to discuss this with your banker and maintain your position as a good manager and a true entrepreneur.

Cash Management

Cash management means managing the balance sheet. Peter Drucker once said: "A business can survive long periods of low earnings if it has adequate cash flow and financial strength. The opposite is not true." Up to now, I have been talking about planning for profits. However, when planning for profits, you must always consider the effect on the balance sheet and your cash position. You may have heard the expression "expanding yourself out of business" many times. Well, this happens when the small-business owner only looks at profits and pays no attention to the effect of expansion on the cash position.

A few years ago, a client of ours who had just come through a difficult time had a great plan for expansion. His bank line of credit was about $100,000 and he was at the limit. His plan was to improve sales by $40,000 per month through a guaranteed promotion program. This was a small manufacturing firm that provided a custom-made product for its customers. His enthusiasm for the project was overwhelming. I found it very difficult to ask some key questions which I knew would dampen this enthusiasm. Nevertheless, I had to ask: What effect would this have on the balance sheet and cash flow? Well, his accounts receivable were running at 60 days ($80,000) and his inventory was running at about 90 days (this was 40% of the selling price) or $48,000. This little expansion of $40,000 in sales per month would require an increase in financing of about $128,000 less any increased accounts payable: accounts receivable ($80,000) and inventory ($48,000).

Needless to say, the expansion program took smaller steps.

Without this planned growth and without recognizing its effect on the balance sheet, I feel quite certain that this company would have found itself in dire financial straits. This means that attention would have been drawn away from running the business to working hand-to-mouth to meet payroll and key suppliers.

What, then, is cash management? In my view, cash management is very simple. You minimize your assets (accounts receivable, inventory, fixed assets) and maximize your liabilities (accounts payable and shareholder's equity). I know this sounds like a paradox, but I would like to refer you to Exhibit 16. This is a comparative balance sheet for this year and last year for Newco Inc. You may recall that the company's profit was $10,000 for the current year. One of the questions that our clients ask most frequently when they have a profit is: "Where did all the cash go?" In this case, the bank loan increased from $10,000 to $40,000, with a $10,000 profit. On the surface, this doesn't make any sense. Let's look at the other parts of the balance sheet. The accounts receivable increased $25,000, inventory increased $20,000, and fixtures and equipment increased $10,000. In other words, the assets increased $55,000. This was offset by an increase in accounts payable of $35,000 and shareholder's equity of $10,000. You will also notice that the note payable was reduced from $40,000 down to $20,000. The net increase in liabilities was $25,000. The bank loan, then, increased by $30,000 due to the increase in assets of $55,000 less the increase in liabilities of $25,000.

Consequently, cash management really means to make the accounts receivable, inventory, and fixed assets as low as possible and to make the accounts payable, notes payable, and shareholder's equity as high as possible (minimize assets, maximize liabilities). When your business starts to grow, you may be quick to suggest that you have cash-flow problems. In some cases, the problems can be the result of under-capitalization. However, in many cases, your cash-flow problems are symptoms. The true cause is poor cash management and the lack of time taken to manage the balance sheet.

EXHIBIT 16

NEWCO INC.
BALANCE SHEET
($000's omitted)

Assets

	Change	This Year	Last Year
Current Assets			
Accounts receivable	$+25	$ 75	$ 50
Inventory	+20	80	60
Prepaid expenses	—	5	5
Fixtures and Equipment	+10	30	20
	$+55	$190	$135

Liabilities and Shareholders' Equity

	Change	This Year	Last Year
Current Liabilities			
Accounts payable	$+35	$ 60	$ 25
Notes payable within one year	—	20	20
Accrued expenses	—	10	10
Notes Payable	−20	20	40
Total liabilities	+15	150	95
Shareholders' Equity	+10	40	30
	$+25	$150	$125
Due to Bank	$+30	$ 40	$ 10

Minimizing Assets

Accounts Receivable

Let's look at minimizing accounts receivable. "A sale is not completed until the cash is collected." Some of you will be more concerned about getting the sale than getting the money. You may suggest that the sale is completed when the customer signs on the dotted line. To emphasize the differences in the management of accounts receivable, let's look at the *Robert Morris & Associates Annual Statement Studies, 1988* and compare the accounts receivable turnovers for "Wholesalers General Merchandise" (SIC 5199). The accounts receivable turnover is set out in three categories: upper quartile (twenty-fifth percent best); average (fifty percent best); and lower quartile (seventy-fifth percent). The respective accounts receivable turnovers are 16.9, 9.9, and 6.6. If we compare this to Newco Inc. where the turnover was 8, then we will discover that this is lower than the average of 9.9. We will also realize that if we were able to maintain the upper quartile turnover of 16.9, then our accounts receivable would be $36,000 ($600,000 divided by 16.9) and this is $39,000 lower than the $75,000 on the Newco balance sheet. By accomplishing this goal, there would be virtually no bank loan.

It is also interesting to note that if Newco was in the lower quartile of 6.6 turns then the accounts receivable would be about $90,000 and the bank loan would be $15,000 more or $55,000. How, then, do you go about minimizing your accounts receivable?

Credit Control
This is done by establishing a credit control. A credit control is a three-step program: credit policy; collections; and bookkeeping.

First, establish a credit policy suitable for your industry. This means defining the terms on which you will sell your product to your customers. Keep in mind that this is an interest-free loan. Your credit policy should include payment terms (a discount if paid within 10 days, for example; the face value of the invoice amount if it is paid before 30 days; COD; et cetera); credit limits for various customers (rate customers on their financial stability, establish credit limits, and review them on a regular basis); and action required for new customers (COD, credit application forms, bank references). Take the time to check your new customers by having a form completed with bank and suppliers' references before any shipments are made.

Collection Procedures

The next, and most important part of your credit-management program, is to establish a firm collection procedure. Before you do that, make sure you know where accounts stand by getting an "aged" accounts receivable trial balance, described in Chapter 9. Be sure you get this within three days after each month-end.

For all customers who haven't paid after 30 days, you should automatically send off a statement. Each morning, take your current accounts receivable trial balance and cross off payments received. On the fifteenth of the month, a designated staff member should phone customers with unpaid accounts in the 30-Day, 60-Day, 90-Day, and over-90 Day columns on the aged accounts receivable trial balance. This person should be trained to be direct, polite, and firm and know how to ask for the overdue account. It's important to get a commitment and write the date of the proposed payment on the customer's record sheet. If the payment has not been received by the commitment date, then telephone again. Remember, he or she has reneged on two commitments to you: your credit policy of 30 days as well as the second commitment. Another commitment date should be determined and written on the customer's collection record. If payment has still not been received by this second commitment date, then you should telephone personally. At this time, you should consider a stop shipment, a COD policy, or a new credit base which is called CBD (cash before delivery).

If you find that you are getting the runaround, send a firm demand letter with a deadline for payment. If the payment is not received on that date, then have the guts to follow through with a writ. Many of these accounts will fall into the small claims court category. This means that you can prepare the claim yourself and file it in the local county court office. Small claims courts provide a convenient and inexpensive forum for deciding claims up to $3,000. There is a nominal filing fee of $17 to $50, depending on the claim and the number of defendants. Interest and legal costs can be added to the claim.

Once you have filed your claim with the court office, the court will inform your customer of your claim. The only way you're likely to be arguing your case in front of a judge is if your customer disputes your claim. If he or she doesn't, and you show the judge enough evidence to convince the judge that your claim is valid, and the customer still doesn't pay, you can obtain a judgment against him or her which is enforceable by a sheriff. But you may not have to go this far. About 50% of those who receive notice of your action will either pay the full amount or offer an acceptable compromise.

Poor collection procedures result in higher interest costs, bad debts, and possibly a cash bind. Particular attention should be given to your larger customers who are just as vulnerable to failure as anyone else. You should review your accounts receivable listing to determine if any one customer represents more than 10% of the outstanding balance. The failure of a small customer will cause a ripple effect. But a big customer will cause a tidal wave that can sink your ship. Therefore, you must maintain a very hard line on collections. Good customers who need your service or product will understand and appreciate your collection policy. If they don't, then they are not good customers.

The third step is to maintain accurate bookkeeping records as mentioned in Chapter 9: sales, receivables, and cash receipts control. It's important to make certain that sales invoices are issued either the day of the shipment or no later than the next day. Be sure the accounts receivable records are updated daily to be certain that none of your customers exceeds his or her allotted credit limit. Your credit policy should be typewritten on one page and copies given to all staff.

Inventory Management
Whether you are in the manufacturing, wholesaling, or retailing industry sectors, you will be quick to learn that controlling your inventory can be the short-term and long-term key to your survival. The banker is usually only interested in using between 25% to 50% of your inventory of raw material and finished goods for margining your bank loan. If you have a bad mix of inventory on hand, then you have non-financeable assets that will require additional profits, capi-

tal injection on your part, or extension of accounts payable to finance. The fact is, poor inventory control can be a killer.

GPROI

In the past, business owners have taken an overall approach to inventory management. In the retail sector, for example, if the inventory turns over four times a year, retailers feel they are doing a good job. However, we all know that some inventory will be turning over once and some will be turning over up to nine times or more. This is the last time that we will refer to inventory turnover because it really doesn't mean anything. The third-wave approach to inventory management is to determine the gross profit return on inventory (GPROI). You are in business to make a profit; therefore, emphasis should relate to profitability, including inventory. The method of calculating the GPROI was set out earlier in this chapter where we indicated that a 300% return was a good target. That means that for every dollar invested in inventory, you should receive three dollars per year of gross profit. That's before paying for wages, occupancy, or other expenses.

However, the overall GPROI also doesn't mean much unless you can have breakdowns by product grouping. We can all take the example of Pareto's Law that 20% of your inventory will represent 80% of your sales and profits. So you need to know which items are included in the 20% and cut back on the 80% to provide you only 20% of your volume. The other major reason for having breakdowns of inventory by product grouping is that when you decide that you need to cut back on inventory, you will know what areas require cutback. There is no point in cutting back on stock that you are selling and making a good profit on because you will only find yourself with empty shelves.

Here is a simple system:

1. Establish the general product categories for your own specific business.
2. Record the purchases of inventory during the month by product category.
3. Determine a cost percentage by product category, record

your sales by the same groupings during the month, and calculate the cost of sales by each category by multiplying the sales by the cost percentage. (This eliminates the necessity of taking the physical inventory every month. However, if it is convenient to take inventory every month, then do so and record it by product category.)

4. Calculate your month-end inventory by product group by adding the opening inventory, the purchases, and subtracting the cost of sales as calculated in number three above.
5. Calculate the GPROI for each of the categories, using annualized gross profit. Annualized gross profit is calculated by taking the actual gross profit for the period, dividing by the number of months involved, and multiplying by twelve.

Let's look at Exhibit 17 "Gross Profit and Inventory Analysis." This type of report can be prepared on a regular basis throughout the year and will indicate gross profit and inventory by product grouping. In this case, we assume that there are four product groupings: A, B, C, and D. You will notice that the gross profits and the GPROI vary considerably by the various product groupings. The advantage of this analysis is that you know generally where the inventory reduction is required. The next step is to analyze the detailed inventory items contained in product groups B and C. If a proper inventory control system is set up as set out in Chapter 9, then this will be relatively simple. However, if a control system is not in place, then a detailed analysis of the inventory on hand must be performed. This can be done by eyeballing the categories and taking specific counts of items that appear to have excess inventory. After the count, the next step is to review purchase invoices for the last two months or so to determine quantities purchased. If one product has thirty items on hand and there were no purchases in the last two months, then this could be considered one of your slow movers and possibly should be eliminated from your product line, returned to the supplier, or sold at a discounted rate to get it off the shelf.

A retail client whose GPROI was about 110% overall

obtained the information by product groups and discovered that one area had a GPROI of 95%. On analyzing the detail, the client discovered that 60 of the 300 items included in the category had six or fewer sales in the past twelve months.

EXHIBIT 17

NEWCO INC.
GROSS PROFIT AND INVENTORY ANALYSIS
($000's omitted)

| | Product Categories | | | | |
	A	B	C	D	Total
Sales	$150	$100	$150	$200	$600
Cost of Sales	120	70	96	114	400
Gross Profit	$ 30	$ 30	$ 54	$ 86	$200
Gross Profit %	20%	30%	36%	43%	33%
Inventory	$ 10	$ 26	$ 28	$ 16	$ 80
GPROI	300%	115%	193%	538%	250%
Target GPROI 300%					
Inventory	$ 10	$ 10	$ 18	$ 16	$ 54
Turns	12X	7X	5X	7X	7X
Target Inventory Reduction	—	16	10	—	26

Armed with some key facts, you then have some decisions to make. In some cases, this is not a simple process as you would probably like to provide total service to your customers. But at least you have an opportunity to make a decision with the available information, knowing that you are probably losing money on these product lines or the specific products within the product line. The secret is not to get caught in the full-line trap.

Exhibit 17 indicates that if each of the four products had a GPROI of at least 300 percent, then the resulting inventory would be $54,000 or $26,000 less than the current. If you do not feel that you can attain these levels, with some effort you can at least expect that the $26,000 reduction could be 50% or, say, $13,000.

Fixed Assets

Effective management of the fixed assets is another key cash-management item. You must remember that one of the main advantages of being a small-business owner is that you have flexibility. You are a creator of new jobs and an employer and when things get tough, you can always cut back. However, if you purchase a fixed asset, you must live with the decision for a long time and you will find it very difficult to reverse. Consequently, do not get caught up in the false saving of purchasing or leasing capital assets to save employees' time or to reduce the cost of outside contractors. (By the way, when you lease equipment, you have bought it.) No doubt, when you perform a feasibility study of cost savings, you can usually justify the purchase. But do not lose sight of the fact that this reduces your flexibility and could be draining your cash required for working capital.

Consider the example of the small-business owner who was fabricating a line of machine products. The owner commenced business by subcontracting many of the component parts and was basically considered an assembly operation. The company reexamined the cost of the subcontractors versus the cost of producing the component parts in-house. The economics indicated that the owner should move to the in-house operation. Within six months, the company was in the hands of a receiver. Although the individual costs were lower, the company was required to purchase raw materials and produce about a two-year supply of the component parts in the first six months in order to make production cost effective. This, together with the cost of the equipment, caused the company's demise. In other words, the owner only considered managing the profit-and-loss statement and gave no consideration to the balance sheet.

The by-product of increased fixed assets is that your debt-to-equity ratio will be higher and your current ratio will be lower, and no doubt your banker will be taking a harder look at the financing package.

Two common examples of misuse of capital funds are purchasing your own vehicle for deliveries and purchasing a piece of equipment to produce components faster. Curb you ego. You don't really need trucks roaming the streets with your name on them. There is an old expression I like to use: Do what you know and what you don't know, buy. If you are manufacturing widgets, why get into the cartage business? It is smart to direct your efforts to your prime target—making widgets—and to allow the specialists to deliver your product. You will pay a premium, but this is more than offset by the time that you will save by not having to administer the cartage operation (hiring, firing, supervising, vehicle maintenance, et cetera) and the capital that would be tied up in the equipment.

Another suggestion is to examine all component parts of your widget and get some prices from firms specializing in the various items. No doubt subcontractors with specialized equipment can produce the components at the same or lower cost. Now you can increase sales without additional equipment and personnel. This should also improve your bottom line and your working-capital position.

The major advantage of subcontractors is that they are usually owner-managed, like your firm, and want to provide the same enthusiastic service. Some of your demands for efforts above and beyond the ordinary may be better received by them than by some of your own staff. In some cases, it may not be practical to use subcontractors, but I would examine this possibility at the outset and as a last resort, do it myself.

A quotation from Dr. Rein Peterson's book, *Building a Balanced Economy*, is appropriate: "Where it has been fashionable for a company to boast how many workers it employs and therefore how powerful it was, it will become fashionable henceforth to boast how much work it has subcontracted out and how much more profitable it is."*

---

* Dr. Rein Peterson, *Building a Balanced Economy* (Toronto: Press Porcepic Ltd., 1977).

Maximizing Liabilities

Accounts Payable

In general terms, managing accounts payable means to drag out payments to suppliers as long as possible. There is a danger in doing this, however, if it is not done properly. You must know your suppliers and, where possible, negotiate longer terms, as discussed in Chapter 6. A common misconception should be debunked: Don't take a 2% cash discount and pay your bill in 10 days. Let's look at an example of a company that is borrowing from the bank at a rate of, say, 14%. Fourteen percent per annum is equivalent to .0384 percent per day (14% divided by 365). Two percent represents fifty-two days (2.0 divided by .0384). Therefore, if you can extend the payment to over 62 days (52 days plus the 10 days grace), then the saving in bank interest will be more than the 2% cash discount. If we can assume that you purchased goods in month one and you pay on the 25th day of month three, then the total days are as follows: one month, 15 days (average); month two, 30 days; month three, 25 days; or 70 days. By paying before the end of month three, you will not be on your supplier's "bad" list. If you maintain a steady payment schedule at this rate, then the supplier will probably go along with you in the long run. However, there will be cases when this is not appropriate, and you need your suppliers, so don't ruffle their feathers too much.

Increasing long-term liabilities in the form of notes payable or debentures is an appropriate way of financing for the long term, especially if it is not locked in to your bank loan, which can be called in difficult times. I should caution that you do not want long-term loans if you are not borrowing short term from the bank. There is no point in paying interest out at a couple of points above prime if you have money deposited which attracts a couple of points under prime.

Shareholders' Equity

Improving your shareholders' equity is the last cash-management technique which generally means an increase in profits. Details of this technique are covered in various chapters in this book.

11

PROFIT PLANNING

Dun & Bradstreet's *Classification of Causes of Business Failures in Canada* suggests that 38% of all failures are caused by inadequate sales. The four major reasons for inadequate sales are identified as: poor quality control; poor promotion; poor sales technique; and poor pricing strategy. Quality control generally relates to the quality of service you are providing to your customers through your employees. This was dealt with in Chapter 7. Promotion and sales techniques were dealt with in Chapter 8. This chapter will deal with pricing strategy.

Three features that can be offered to customers are high quality, good service, and low price; but to make a reasonable profit, all three cannot be offered at the same time. Small-business owners who provide high quality and good service cannot offer low prices as well. However, if you choose to have low quality or poor service, then you may have no alternative but to sell at a lower price.

It is fair to say that most small-business owners, especially in the start-up stage, lack the confidence to charge a reasonable price for their products or services. They are often caught up in getting the order and building the business and client base. It's true that to get those initial orders, you may have to provide additional service or offer some type of strategic discounting, but you should also make it very clear to your customers that this is a special arrangement. Your customers will, of course, have a short memory and will be quick to review your last invoice prices. In the service industry, and especially in consulting, you may find that many years will go by before you are able to get those initial clients up to your standard charges.

One thing to remember—in fact, to keep uppermost in your mind—is this: If you feel confident that you have a good product or a good service, you deserve reasonable compensation. No doubt, in the first year, your plan will be to survive and get the show on the road. But by the second year, you should be targeting pre-tax profits of about 20% of gross profit and/or 20% to 30% of the operating assets of your business. This means that if your sales total $500,000, if your material cost totals $300,000, and if your resulting gross profit is $200,000, then your net profit should be no less than $40,000 before income taxes (and after you have been paid a reasonable salary for your efforts). The operating assets include accounts receivable, inventory, and the net fixed assets on the balance sheet. If the operating assets total $200,000 (accounts receivable, $50,000; inventory, $100,000; net fixed assets, $50,000), then you should be looking for a profit of between $40,000 and $60,000.

Proper pricing can make or break your small business. If your prices are too high, your sales may be too low; if your prices are too low, your profits may be minimal or they may dwindle to nothing.

In Chapter 5, we discussed the feasibility of your venture. One of the points we emphasized was that you must know what business you are really in. You cannot be everything to everyone. You must target your market and price your products or services accordingly. Among other things, you must know the attitudes of your target market. Are they looking for a deal? Or are they the consumer elite that prefers to buy an item *because* it is higher-priced? There are indeed many people who will compare two products and buy the more expensive one because they reason that it *must* be better. Therefore, if you create a high-quality, upmarket image for your product and claim that it is somehow superior to others of its kind, you won't necessarily have to meet the competition's price.

This chapter will deal with pricing for profit. In many cases this means "guts management." It is important for you, as a new business owner, to have the guts to charge the price that your product or service deserves.

Pricing for Profit

Calculating the Profit Point

In Chapter 5, we discussed the break-even point. As you may already have guessed, it is not good enough to break even. Yes, it is necessary to determine whether the venture is feasible or not, but what you are really in business to do is to meet your target profit. So, it's time to calculate the profit point. If we assume that your profit target is 20% of gross profit, then the profit-point formula is as follows:

$$\frac{\text{Fixed expenses}}{\text{Gross Profit \% } - \text{ 20\% of Gross Profit \%}}$$

The example used in Chapter 5 is a company with monthly fixed expenses of $10,000 and a 25% gross profit. The break-even point is $40,000 in sales per month:

$$\frac{\$10,000}{25\%}$$

The profit point is $50,000 sales per month:

$$\frac{\$10,000}{25\% - 20\% \text{ of } 25\% \text{ (5\%)}}$$

The real task is not to break even at $40,000 in sales per month, but to make a reasonable profit with sales of $50,000 per month. This target should be in sight sometime during the second year of operation; say, by the eighteenth month after your start-up. If $50,000 appears unreasonable, you must go back to the drawing board as you did in Chapter 5 to review the gross profit and the expenses.

Achieving Your Target Profit

If we assume that nothing can be done with the expenses, then the only way to obtain a reasonable target profit is to improve the gross profit. This can be done in three ways: by purchasing or manufacturing the product less expensively; by increasing the selling price; or by increasing the unit sales, which will in all probability reduce the product cost and ultimately, in combination with the latter, improve the actual gross profit.

The simplest approach is, of course, to increase the selling price. If you have determined that $40,000 in sales is feasible by, say, the sixth or seventh month of operation, then the target gross profit should be whatever will allow $40,000 of sales to provide you with a reasonable return. I realize that we are performing a very academic calculation. However, the planning process must start, at least in part, with theory; the numbers are then massaged and changed in light of all of the surrounding information. So bear with me. If the expenses are $10,000 per month; they must be considered to represent 80% of the gross profit in order to attain a 20% target profit. The gross profit should therefore be $12,500 ($10,000 divided by 80 times 100). This is 31.25% of the $40,000 sales. On first review, you will be shocked to see that this is a substantial increase in gross profit over the 25% that was in your initial plan. However, it can be accomplished by a mere 6.25% increase in the selling price (6.25% of $40,000 is $2,500). It is now time to review each of your products and its selling price to determine which can be increased by 6.25%. You may feel comfortable increasing the price of some of your products but not others. In any event, this academic exercise may have revealed some products where the price could safely be increased by 10%. Although you may not attain the full target gross profit of 31.25% of sales, you might be able to increase the overall gross profit to, say, 28%. This would mean that, to achieve the original target profit of $2,500, you would have to *increase* sales to a little under $45,000 a month (as opposed to $50,000). You should constantly review the selling prices and gross profits of the individual products with the target profit in mind. In time, you should attain the pre-tax profit goal of 20% of gross profit. Remember that the long-term success of your small business will be tied to setting profit goals and pricing accordingly.

There are four basic keys to proper pricing: know the market; know the competition; establish company profit goals; and know your costs.

Pricing your product or service is an integral part of your marketing program, regardless of your position in the chain of distribution: manufacturer, broker, wholesaler, or retailer. In Chapter 5, we covered market analysis and the importance of knowing your market and your competition. And we have just discussed how to go about establishing profit goals. The fourth key to proper pricing—knowing your costs—is important, but this key is obvious to retailers, wholesalers, and brokers. However, some manufacturers have problems determining the actual cost of a product. In Chapters 5 and 10, we discussed the use of subcontractors as a way of minimizing costs and, in the short run, this is the best approach. In the long run, no doubt you will wish to set up your own manufacturing facility where you will have total control of production, quality, and delivery to your customers. In this case, you need a simple cost system to establish the actual manufactured cost. It should include materials, direct labor, and the factory overhead of each item you sell. We will discuss cost systems in greater detail later on in the chapter.

Pricing Strategy

Once you have established your standard prices, then you must establish a pricing strategy. It is one of the most important parts of your marketing program. In other words, why will you sell your products for more or less than, say, the standard prices that you have presently established? There are circumstances that you must consider as part of your pricing program. The most important is current profits. As discussed above, your current profits will be directly affected by your pricing strategy. After you have established your standard rates, you may, through experience and further research, discover that you can increase the prices and still maintain the same unit sales. This will increase the gross profit and the ultimate bottom line. Likewise, research may indicate that lowering the price a few percentage points might increase the unit sales substantially and again improve the actual dollar gross profit and the bottom line.

However, as the vice-president of marketing (as well as chief financial officer) for your new venture, you must develop a strategy in order to get your business off the ground. For example, you are virtually entering a new market. You may feel that to penetrate this market you will require a lower price than that of the competition. In other words, potential customers may sidestep the New Company Syndrome if they feel they can obtain the same product and/or service from you for less than the current supplier is charging. Once you have broken the barrier in this way, you must reconsider this policy and move your prices back up to earn your target profits.

The pricing strategy of some new businesses is to build traffic, and to do so, they must offer a deal. For example, we have a client who started up a new restaurant serving larger-than-normal portions at less-than-market prices. He did this for about a year. When the traffic was built up, the prices and the portions gradually fell into line. Because the change was not sudden, the established loyal clientele were not upset. The restaurant is now a thriving, mature new business.

Once your business is established, your pricing strategy will continue to be affected by the competition. You may have to ward off new entries into your market area. This could mean either meeting their price or reducing your price even further to keep them out.

Part of your pricing strategy may be to stick with the standard prices and increase your market share or build traffic by providing a high-quality product along with excellent service. You may find that the lower-priced competition will be nibbling at your heels. However, if they provide the same quality and excellent service at a lower price, they may have difficulty staying in business.

Let's look at some specific pricing strategies for retailers. Retailers must define the image they wish to project to their customers. Some very prosperous retailers have succeeded with loss-leader pricing strategy. One example is Ed Mirvish's store, Honest Ed's. Everyone shopping there feels that he or she is getting a deal. Tremendous line-ups can be seen before opening when a product normally sold for five dollars is on sale for two dollars (the offer is usually limited to two per customer). This has proven very successful, but it doesn't necessarily work for everyone. There has been a proliferation of wholesale retailers in the 1980s. One area is the wholesale drug-mart concept. If you look at the financial papers, you will find that one of the prominent entries in the field has very low profits and a very low return on investment. You will also notice that Shoppers Drug Mart has folded all of its Howie's wholesale drug marts into the Shoppers Drug Mart network. You will also read from time to time about the receivership or bankruptcy of others. In other words, the trend in the early 1980s was the concept of wholesaling at the retail level. But profitability was questionable.

If you intend to establish a full-service, no-discount quality business for the upscale market, you will also discover that you will be stuck with certain products at the end of the season. You can be sure of one thing: your snob clientele is not interested in buying last year's styles. A good strategy, in this case, is to consider end-of-season sales directed at your key clientele in order to reduce your investment in inventory. However, if you intend to operate a high-volume, low gross-profit discount operation, then you will no doubt be having continuous sales or discounts, and your clientele will always think that it is getting a deal.

In many cases, wholesalers' selling prices may be dictated by their manufacturing suppliers. However, they may wish to establish prices that include quantity discounts. In other words, buy 10 at the standard price, but 20 at a 5% quantity discount. This strategy can be used very well in order to minimize the number of shipments to customers and to improve overall sales. If the customer is a retailer, he or she may take the discount as additional income or may possibly pass it on to the customer in an effort to improve unit sales.

Manufacturers' pricing strategies are more comprehensive

than those of retailers or wholesalers because they must determine a reasonable selling price to the end user as well as determining the gross profit required by the middlemen. This was discussed in Chapter 5. Much of their concern will be with the quantities of a product that can be sold; that is, with economies of scale. In other words, if they can sell 10,000 units, the unit manufacturing cost will be much less than if they were to sell 1,000. The manufacturer is required to establish the costs of the individual products being produced at various sales levels. It is possible that in the first year or two, the ultimate pricing to the wholesaler will provide only a 20% gross profit, for example. Once the market is established and the quantities increase, the cost will go down through economies of scale. This should increase the manufacturer's gross profit to the target of 30%.

Manufacturing Cost
One major problem with small-business manufacturing is that owners are often wrong about the costs of manufacturing their products and, sadly, set selling prices based on inaccurate information. This inaccuracy can set off an unhappy chain of events: goods are improperly priced, gross margins are lower than estimated, profits are reduced or losses are sustained and, eventually, the operation fails.

This is frequently the result of not having a simple but proper costing system implemented from the outset to determine the actual costs of production, including the cost of materials, labor, and the plant overhead.

When smoking was fashionable, manufacturers' costing systems could often be found on the back of their cigarette pack. The current approach tends to involve the back of a scratch pad, where an owner arbitrarily writes down figures for the estimated material, the labor, and the factory overhead percentage. One thing is certain: this approach is inaccurate and invariably underestimates costs. For example, ad hoc calculations of materials will not take into account waste and reruns. The owner will tend to measure labor requirements on the basis of his or her own abilities, forgetting that employees are not likely to apply themselves with the same enthusiasm and ambition.

Another major costing problem is the accurate calculation of the factory overhead rate or the "burden rate." Factory overhead includes rent, insurance, equipment, depreciation, factory supplies, employee benefits, maintenance and repairs, and "indirect plant labor." It is normally calculated by dividing the total factory overhead by the direct plant labor times 100. For example, if the direct plant labor is $100,000 and the factory overhead is $50,000, then the overhead rate is fifty percent. The fallacy of this academic calculation is that a portion of the direct plant labor will be indirect labor, which is part of overhead. Without accurate costing information, the owner will never know.

Here is an example of what can happen without accurate costing information. If you estimate that your material costs according to the specifications are $40, the direct labor is $20, and the factory overhead (50% of the direct labor, because that's what shows in your financial statements) is $10, then the total is $70. If your company's objective is 35% gross profit, then the selling price is $108 ($70 divided by 65 times 100).

The major problem with an ad hoc costing system, however, is that the labor and factory overheads are usually underestimated. In my experience, in implementing cost systems, I have discovered that if the total plant labor is 100, then the direct labor is no more than 75%. This means that 25% of the total is, in fact, indirect labor and should be included as factory overhead. The 25% indirect labor is taken up by shipping, receiving, storing, waiting for a job, washroom trips, coffee breaks, and so on. If your business plan indicates that the annual factory direct labor will be $500,000, and the factory overhead is $250,000, then it may seem fair to assume that the overhead rate is 50%. A proper costing system would reduce the direct plant labor by the indirect labor, which will be in the area of $125,000 (25% of $500,000). This should be deducted from the direct labor costs of $500,000 and will result in a net plant labor of $375,000. Similarly, the factory overhead of $250,000 will be increased by $125,000 to $375,000. The resulting overhead rate is actually 100%, not 50%.

Going back to the example, then, if the resulting actual

cost is material $40, direct labor $25 ($5 more than estimated), and factory overhead $25, then the total cost is $90. This results in a gross profit of 16%, not 35%. In order to obtain the 35% gross profit, the selling price would have to be about $139 ($90 divided by 65 times 100). This is one major reason why there are 80% failures in start-ups in manufacturing concerns.

This problem can be easily resolved by implementing a simple labor distribution system. Various alternatives exist, but a simple approach is to assign a number to each work order and to have the plant personnel record the amount of time spent on each work order on a daily time report. These time reports go to the office every day. The details are recorded on the job-cost records or dockets for each work order. The details can be converted to dollars at the appropriate employees' rates in total as jobs are completed.

An alternative approach is to use an average daily labor rate of all plant personnel, record the time, and make one calculation at the completion of the job. The plant foreman or you must monitor these job time charges and report the totals of charge hours and noncharge hours daily. The total charge hours and noncharge hours are summarized at the end of each month, and the dollar value is calculated and recorded as plant direct labor and plant overhead cost. In my experience, I have found that the ratio is 75% direct charge time and 25% noncharge time.

The result of this simple procedure is that all time spent by the plant staff is accounted for through the payroll records and charged to the various jobs, products, and indirect labor. This pinpoints the actual direct labor cost for each job or product. Estimating and bidding will become more accurate as you build such cost files.

Once you have established the costs for the various products, then the cost system should continue so you can compare the future actual performance to the standard. If you find that the costs are increasing for the same product, then it is time to go back to the drawing board and determine why. One reason may be inefficiency and low productivity on the part of your staff. If there are signs that the plant personnel are loafing, then you must determine the necessary course of action to motivate the staff for improved productivity. This was dealt with in Chapter 7: Human Resources. However, increased costs may derive from an increase in labor rates and material costs due to inflation. If the actual costs are increasing, then you must review your selling prices to achieve the gross profit in your business plan. But before you increase prices, you must review your competition and review your pricing strategy. The cost system in your manufacturing operation will become the key information source for short- and long-term decisions.

Pricing Pitfalls

I have noticed over the years that many small-business owners operate without proper information and make decisions by the seat of their pants. To a great degree, these decisions are emotional ones based on hearsay and how they feel that particular day. If business is bad, the first reaction is to cut prices and avoid disaster. If business is good, they decide to lower prices and get a greater share of the market. There is nothing wrong with either one of these decisions if they are calculated and based on facts. Unfortunately, they are often ad hoc decisions, made emotionally, and they result in lower profits or losses. In many cases, these decisions may even cause failures.

Many small-business owners do not make a reasonable profit for their investment, their personal effort, and the risk involved in owning and managing a small business. The main reason is underpricing of their products or services.

There are several reasons for underpricing. The first is the fear of losing a sale. This is sometimes uppermost in the small-business owner's mind. In the case of some service companies, such as consulting firms, there is a strong fear of losing the customer as well.

Another reason is laziness. Let's face it: it's easier to sell a high-priced item at a discount than to do a good selling job and get full list price. Laziness extends itself into what is referred to as mark-up pricing. Some automatically calculate the selling price by using the industry standards. For example, gift stores usually operate on the "keystone" method (mark-up 100%). I recently encountered a gift-store owner who had a gross profit of 47%, where the industry norm is about 37%. In addition, he was making reasonable profits of 20% of gross profit, whereas the industry was more in the 5% area. His main secret to success is that he takes the time to research the market for the individual new products and prices them accordingly, not necessarily "keystone." In some cases, he will price a $10 item at $24.99 instead of $19.99. This is a 60% gross profit. This approach is successful and will go a long way to decreasing the profit point. In addition, the increase in gross profit on these items will offset some of the future gross-profit reductions that are necessary in order to move slow-moving or end-of-season inventory.

The other reasons for underpricing are due to incorrect costing information and failure to establish target profits, as described earlier.

The best approach is to shore up your security. Don't sell yourself short.

Discounting: A Give-Away Program
Some of the advocates of discounting for the sake of increased volume do not realize the actual consequences of their decision. They fail to ask themselves: "How great an increase in sales do I have to achieve to make up for the loss in gross profit that comes with decreasing my selling price by ten percent?" Here is the formula:

$$\frac{\text{Gross profit }\%}{\text{Gross profit }\% - 10\%} = \times \frac{\text{the current}}{\text{unit volume}} = \frac{\text{increased}}{\text{unit volume}}$$

Let us assume, then, that gross profit is 35% and the current unit sales per year are 1,000. If the items are selling for $100 each, then the annual gross profit is $35,000. If the selling price is reduced by 10%, then the number of units required to be sold to maintain the same dollar gross profit is 1,400 units.

$$\frac{35}{25\ (35\ -\ 10)} \times 1,000 = 1,400 \text{ units}$$

Selling 1,400 at $90 with a $25 gross profit equals $35,000 of annual gross profit. A quick calculation suggests that this is a 40% increase in the unit sales to accommodate a 10% decrease in selling price.

The next question is "Can I sell 1,400 units at this lower price?" If the answer is no, then discounting makes no sense. If, however, you feel that you can sell more than 1,400 units without increasing the operating expenses, then go ahead. By the way, none of this takes into account the image that you are trying to create with your customers.

The bullish approach is to say: "What happens if I increase my selling price by ten percent?" In this case, the formula changes as follows:

$$\frac{\text{Gross profit \%}}{\text{Gross profit \% + 10\%}} \times \text{current unit sales} = \text{unit sales}$$

In this case, the number of units required to be sold to provide the same dollar gross profit is 778:

$$\frac{35}{45\% \ (35\% + 10\%)} \times 1,000 = 778 \text{ units}$$

By selling 778 units (78% of current sales) at $110 each, with a gross profit of $45 each, your overall gross profit is maintained at $35,000.

Hence, if you consider yourself part of the upscale market and your product can stand a 10% increase in price, you only need to sell 778 units.

And if you have defined your company image as high-volume, low gross profit, you must decide whether you can sell 1,400 units versus 1,000 units at the lower price.

There are many small-business owners who have neither defined their company image, nor developed a corresponding overall pricing strategy. They tend to drift and go with the flow. Discounting at the retail level must be conducted on a planned basis, with an overall objective in mind. Ad hoc sales and discounts do nothing but reduce profits. In fact, in my view, discounting is usually a give-away program.

Cautionary Tales

Let's look at how a few types of small businesses approach the pricing of their products or services.

The story of one wholesaler, who started up on the premise that his gross profit was 30%, provides a classic example of a common pricing problem. This calculation of the break-even point and the profit point had indicated that his business was a feasible venture. The operational plan indicated reasonable profits in the first year. After three months in operation, the monthly financial reports indicated that the sales and expenses were on target but that the inventory was increasing. The monthly financial statements were prepared on the basis of using costing factors. In other words, the sales were recorded by product and an estimated cost-of-sales percentage was determined for each product group, and these costing factors were used to record the cost of sales. The inventory by the various product groups was determined by recording the purchases by these groups and reducing it by the estimated cost at the end of each month. The increase in the book value of the inventory indicated either that the costing factors were wrong or that excess inventory was being purchased. The owner informed us that the inventory was virtually the same as in the previous months. The investigation brought to light the fact that the mark-up, not the gross profit, was 30%. The gross profit was in fact only 23%. The owner had confused the term *mark-up* with *gross profit* and had based his projections on an erroneous premise.

Don't confuse gross profit percentage with mark-up percentage. The former is the ratio of the gross profit to *sales*; the latter is the ratio of gross profit to *cost of sales*. In this example, the selling price would have been, say one dollar, and the cost $0.77. The gross profit was, therefore, $0.23 or 23% (0.23 divided by 100). The mark-up percentage was 30 (0.23 divided by 0.77 times 100).

Another example of a pricing miscalculation involved an individual who had been dehired and was going to establish a consulting firm in the area of his expertise. He got the idea, talked to respective people in the industry, received favorable feedback, and decided to proceed with the business. It was simple to start up, as he planned to work out of his house, and all he required was an answering service, cards, and letterhead. My first question was: "What is your charge rate?" The answer was $30 per hour. He figured that 1,500 working hours per year at $30 would mean $45,000 of annual income, less minimal expenses. This would be very nice. What this gentleman failed to realize was that time is required for marketing, administration, and some charge time that can't be billed to the customer. In fact, as a sole practitioner in any consulting firm, the number of hours that can be billed in a year is closer to 800–1,000. From that you must deduct all of the operating expenses. Remember that you will be paying your own Canada Pension Plan, auto, and any promotional expenses that might be necessary. After a brief discussion, the gentleman realized that his net profit for the year would be in the area of $25,000. This realization came as quite a shock.

If you are contemplating starting a consulting business, you must first determine your profit objectives as you would in any other business. If you will be working out of your house, then you can still expect between $5,000 and $10,000 of expenses for your business. If your target earnings are, say, $60,000, then your billings must be, say, $70,000, and your charge rate, between $85 and $90 per hour. Some of you may be shocked by such high hourly rates. However, review your last job. Add up your salary and benefits, including CPP, UIC, and the health benefit program. Next, calculate the number of hours per year that you were at work. There are at least ten working days of holidays, possibly ten to twenty-five days of vacation, sick leave, professional-development courses, training conferences, and so forth. If we can assume that the total working days are 220 at seven hours, the total hours are 1,440. By the way, this does not include afternoons taken off for baseball games, two-to-three hour lunches, and personal time. The odds are, it is more like 1,440. If your salary was $60,000 and, say, 10% for benefits, then your total direct cost to the company was about $66,000, which is about $47 per hour ($66,000 divided by 1,440). In your position as an executive or middle manager in a company, you would have had support staff and an overhead of at least 50%, but more likely 100%, of your cost.

At 100%, your cost to the company, including overhead, was about $94 per hour. If your company was to hire you on a per-diem basis of, say, $85 an hour, it would probably be getting a good deal. In fact, you might be surprised to discover that some of your former colleagues may well be doing consulting work for the old firm on an hourly basis.

Pricing pitfalls are also commonly encountered in the restaurant business. I was involved as a consultant for a restaurant in the mid-1970s. Some of you may recall that there was a tremendous increase in the price of meat (beef, pork, poultry, et cetera) at that time. The main reason for the increase was the shortage of protein for feed, which caused the cost of feed to escalate. The main reason for the shortage of protein confirmed that we were in a global economy even at that point: the key ingredients—soya beans and anchovies—were scarce. President Nixon paid subsidies to farmers not to grow soya beans, and the anchovies missed their annual swim to the shores of Peru. Meat prices increased because the cost of feed accounted for about 75% of the cost of raising chickens, cattle, and other livestock.

During this time, I was happy to see my client, the owner of a restaurant, increasing the price of his beef sandwiches virtually every week. Granted, it made for a messy menu, but the owner knew his costs, had a pricing policy, had target profits, and knew what the price had to be in order to attain his profit goals. Although I had to pay more for the sandwich each week, I could do nothing but applaud this true entrepreneur who clearly had control over his company. I might also add that many restaurants failed during this time because they didn't keep up with their rising costs.

In the early 1980s another restauranteur contacted me because he felt there were some problems with his operation. He suggested that his bookkeeping was inaccurate because it indicated a lower gross profit than he had originally planned. To check the figures, it was necessary to calculate the actual food and alcohol costs, which we did. This was done by taking a physical count, and pricing the inventory at the beginning and the end of the week by product groups. The actual product used was the opening inventory, plus the purchases for the week, less the closing inventory. Actual sales by product groups were also recorded during that week. The actual food-cost percentages were the same as those noted in the accounting records. In other words, the problem lay in the pricing: the owner had not kept up with his costs, and his products were underpriced. After some discussion, we were able to convince him to increase his prices accordingly and have new menus printed. As a result, none of his customers noticed the increase. Our client was back on track.

The secret to making a profit in a restaurant operation is to have a detailed cost system which, in fact, involves costing out the recipe for each item on the menu. And if a recipe calls for a four-ounce slice of ham or beef (or whatever), no more than four ounces should be served. Each kitchen should have a small scale for periodic checking of weights. The costing of recipes should be updated each time any invoice comes in that shows an increase in food cost. The restaurant that survives does its homework and knows where it stands. This is one of the reasons that franchised food-service operations have a better chance of surviving than do independent start-ups: the basic controls are in place at the outset.

A final example of a pricing pitfall involves an import-export company that acquired the Canadian rights to import a specialty item. All of the bases were covered for the company's start-up, including costing. The target profit was determined, the necessary gross profit calculated, and a selling price to the wholesalers decided upon. Promotional material was printed, and some television advertising was in place to launch the product. When the first shipment arrived, duty and federal sales tax were charged in the amounts expected. The only problem was that this particular item attracted excise tax, for which the owner had not been prepared. It amounted to only $0.10 a unit, but the company was selling the unit for $1.00. All of a sudden, then, the $0.70 cost that was to produce a 30% gross profit jumped to $0.80, allowing only a 20% gross profit. At this point, it was too late to increase the selling price to the end user, as the packaging, point-of-sale display, advertising, and promotional materials all bore the original selling price. By the way, it was, ironically, the selling price that had been considered the only questionable item in the marketing plan: it was thought to be too high. The fact is, this venture was not feasible.

Examples of the pitfalls in starting up businesses abound. However, I would like to end this chapter on a positive note. If you do your homework as we suggested, and cover all the bases, and this includes having comprehensive discussions with your advisors, the odds are that you will not have to face any of these disastrous results.

12

COMPUTERS AND YOUR BUSINESS

Computers have spearheaded the third wave: the age of technology. In the 1960s, computers were strictly for big business. The cost of hardware was prohibitive for small business and, quite frankly, this new technology was scary. Who needs to lose control of his company and put it in the hands of computer programmers and analysts? The 1970s saw the introduction of the mini computer, which became somewhat affordable to small-business owners. During the 1970s, some adventurous small-business owners took the leap and bought computers, only to discover that they were not the magic wands they were advertised to be. These expensive pieces of hardware required another important element: software. Throughout Canada and the United States, many computers ended up as white elephants.

In some cases, small-business owners were on the brink of bankruptcy (some, indeed, stepped over it), as a result of the disruption that the new equipment caused, and the lack of timely information needed to manage the business that ensued. Although the failure of any business can usually be attributed to poor management on the part of the owner, I would venture to suggest that many of these failures were the result of progressive small-business owners being hoodwinked and conned into purchasing these magic wands that were supposed to solve all of their problems.

The computer salesmen deserve much of the credit for

these failures and the downturns of many of their customers. Their job was to sell the hardware, collect the money, and get out fast. In some cases, sharp salesmen figured out their customers' budgets. They then recommended the computer configuration that would fit the budgets, but not necessarily the needs, of the small-business owner.

Microcomputers and Their Small-Business Applications
Then along came the 1980s and the entry of the fabulous personal computer (PC) or microcomputer. This and the better software packages revolutionized the use of computers in business. The drop in prices enabled even the smallest of the small businesses to purchase a computer and utilize it to advantage. It was the key to providing the necessary information to manage the business.

Many small-business owners have taken advantage of this new technology. A survey conducted by one of the national Canadian chartered banks in 1988 indicates that sixty-five percent of small businesses (classified as those under $2,000,000 in sales) have microcomputers in place. The educational system has made many graduates from the public-school system computer-oriented. This has eliminated the scare factor. And PCs are referred to as "user friendly." In fact, many of the new entrants into the business community find it difficult to conduct their business affairs without a computer.

The microcomputer has many uses for a business owner from correspondence and reports to commercial uses (inventory control, sales-order systems, et cetera) and general bookkeeping, general ledger, and financial statements. Spreadsheet programs such as Lotus 1-2-3 have provided small-business owners with a flexible vehicle for the planning and preparation of monthly forecasts of income and cash flow. It has allowed the use of "what if" scenarios as part of the planning process.

There is a proliferation of standard programs available; for example, Word Perfect for the word-processor application. ACCPAC and New Views are examples of general-ledger packages which provide ongoing bookkeeping and financial information. There are chains of franchised retail operations selling microcomputers across Canada and the United States. Some governments (for example, the Ontario government) have provided incentives for all training programs that include computers. In the Ontario government's Skills program, up to eighty percent of the training cost is paid for by the government.

The information society is here and has been here for some time now. In the past, the head executives of large companies required assistants to gather information upon which to make decisions. Those human resources have largely been replaced by computers. This is one of the major reasons for the total restructuring and downsizing, and simultaneous increase in productivity, evident today in North American business.

Computers have gone beyond the offices of small business owners. CAD/CAM is here: Computer Assisted Design and Computer Assisted Manufacturing. We have architectural and engineering clients who are utilizing computers in place of drafting personnel. The results are lower labor costs, more accurate results and, in the long-term, greater productivity. One of our clients has installed a robot to perform some of the welding functions in his plant. Where five individuals took five hours to complete the task for one unit, the robot, with the assistance of one person, completes the unit in one hour.

My own company has seen the results and the advantages of word-processing systems. We implemented our system in 1978. Before that, we had to type each of our reports, financial statements, and notes to the financial statement. We now need only to input changes. The time saved in keyboarding and proofreading have enabled our company virtually to triple the number of clients we serve without adding typing staff. And our bills for correction fluid have decreased tremendously.

There are numerous uses for the microcomputer. Many of the complicated repetitive details of operating a small business can be handled by a properly installed microcomputer. Don't get me wrong; it's not a magic wand. You may spend six months to a year before you see the results of implementing a computer system. In the long run, you must have a computer in place to process many of the repetitive tasks. These tasks will vary with each company. The secret is to review each activity and to determine which items can be done better by the computer. Although I am excited about the many uses of a computer in small business, I would like to suggest that not every process should be done by the computer. You must examine each procedure and evaluate if the computer can perform the function better and faster than a staff member.

I was involved in a consulting assignment in the mid-1970s that offers a good example of the misapplication of computer technology. The client was a manufacturer of modular furniture, which was becoming very popular for the open-office complex. The owner wanted to implement a computer system that would summarize the various orders to be processed in any given week and schedule the mass production of similar components for these orders. At the time, I questioned the need for this, but the owner was adamant that he wanted to computerize his operation. My job was to act as liaison between the company and the computer programmers. At the start-up date, the various necessary steps were taken to implement the program. Naturally, there were some initial start-up problems and the information that the computer printer spouted out was not accurate. The problems seemed to be resolved very quickly, however, when the assistant plant manager, who had been performing the scheduling in the past, presented a summary of the work to be done. This saved the day. In discussions with this individual, I discovered that it took him two hours to break out the production requirements for the week from the respective orders. The message: Don't use a computer for something that can be done just as easily manually unless there is a tremendous time saving. In other words, two hours a week will never justify the cost and the confusion occasioned by putting all of the production scheduling into the computer.

Here is another example. We were asked by one of the national soft-drink companies if we could prepare a monthly sales report on the various brands of soda pop in litres. The input document to prepare this report was the shipping reports for each truck, each day, and the various sizes of containers. Our job, then, was to input the details from these daily shipping records for each truck and accumulate the data by flavor and respective size of container. However, the standard programming available in our computer was unable to convert the various-sized containers of fluid ounces to litres and then accumulate the information by the flavors. Our first reaction was to consult with a computer programmer who indicated a fee of about $10,000 (that was in 1980 dollars). In discussing this with our computer operator, she came up with a very interesting suggestion. Why not accumulate everything by size and flavor, make about thirty manual calculations, which would take about fifteen minutes, and convert these calculations to the fluid litres on a weekly basis and reinput the figures into our standard program in the computer? The message: don't try to make your computer do everything. There is nothing wrong with supplementing some complex programming with a little manual input.

POS Systems

The computer revolution has arrived for small business retailers as well. Intelligent point-of-sale (POS) systems have begun to transform the way retailers sell and buy merchandise. As I indicated before, inventory can be a killer. POS systems will tell you exactly what the sales activity is for each specific product in your store. No longer will you be coerced into buying a deal that really isn't a deal or overstocking slow-moving products. Retailers are now able to buy only those items that are really selling. The POS is not new to the big guys. Before the microcomputer, only the big chains (grocery stores and other major retailers) could afford POS systems. Now the microcomputer has made POS systems affordable for the little guy.

You will remember Pareto's Law: 80% of your sales and profits come from 20% of your product. Well, there is a follow-up to this: 15% of your sales will come from 15% of your products. This means that 5% of your sales are probably coming from 65% of your inventory. The secret to efficient inventory management is to determine what products comprise that 65% and eliminate or minimize them. After you install a point-of-sale system and it is operating properly, you will be able to obtain detailed information about the activity of each product in your store and make the kinds of informed decisions that will reduce the redundant inventory. Some of the point-of-sale computers will also provide the GPROI by item.

Here is a checklist of some of the benefits that you can expect:

1. The ability to target GPROI by product.
2. An automatic reorder of store inventory.
3. The improved valuation of new product lines. (Should you keep or discontinue them?)
4. Reduced shrinkage.
5. The elimination of price errors (under-rings).
6. Improved personnel scheduling.
7. The elimination of price changes by cashiers.

Such benefits will add up to improved profits and an improved cash position for any retailer.

Computerizing Your Operation

There are numerous uses for the microcomputer in the small-business operation. In fact, if you look at every aspect of your business, you may very well find an application. However, remember the message above. Don't pay for complicated programming when the job can be done very easily on a manual basis. Retailers can use computers for inventory control (POS), the processing of purchases and accounts payable, the preparation of monthly financial statements, and the preparation of financial projections (forecast monthly income statements and forecast monthly cash-flow statements). Wholesalers and manufacturers can utilize computers in similar ways to the retailer, but can also process sales orders, invoices, and accounts receivable. Restaurant operations have computers developed for them that record a customer's order, process it through the computer which automatically records the order in the kitchen, and prepares the necessary customer bill.

With the introduction of the lap-top computer, some salespeople are utilizing computers to process orders during the day. Through a modem, they can send the orders back to the office for processing the next morning. The uses of the computer in the small-business operation will only be curtailed by the lack of imagination about how it may be used to improve productivity, increase controls, and generally increase profits for a small business.

Having said so much that is encouraging, I must now say that you will not obtain the benefits of the computer era without a lot of hard work and careful planning. The value and benefit of your computer will depend on the time and energy you put into using it effectively. If you haven't already joined the computer era, then before you buy one, examine your motives. If your purchase is strictly an ego trip, forget it.

The next step is to list your needs. For example, if you are a retailer and contemplating the purchase of a POS computer, then you may list your needs as set out on page 191. However, these should be reassessed as they may really be your wants. There are many point-of-sale computers that can provide the necessary essential information for you to manage your inventory without necessarily having a detailed inventory system. A POS system that provides you with sales information by product group and product is probably adequate for retailers under $1,000,000. The cost of operating the sales-only data is much less than having a comprehensive inventory-control and automatic-reorder feature that may be part of your wants. In fact, one of our clients who manufactures and sells point-of-sale computers informs us that only one-third of the sales include the inventory-control features. The retail customers are able to monitor the inventory by reviewing the sales data by product.

While you may want financial statements that automatically calculate some of the ratios set out in Chapter 10, in some cases this can be costly custom programming to save five minutes of calculations per month.

Therefore, if you have made a list of your needs, not wants, then the next step is not to purchase the computer, but to examine the available software. Virtually all available software can be used on any IBM-compatible microcomputer. At this point, it may be appropriate to contact your outside accountant to review your plans and have him or her provide some input as to the appropriate software and the computer requirements. This would include ensuring that the software program is purchased from a reputable dealer and there is support from the manufacturer, the dealer, and other facilities for training. There is nothing more frustrating than getting new software with difficult-to-understand manuals from a dealer who is "here today, gone tomorrow," with no formal training programs available.

Once you have decided on the software, the hardware is the next choice. It is easy to go overboard and buy the most expensive (or the least expensive) computer. Keep this in mind: your computer will probably be obsolete within one year, so don't exceed two years in any payback calculations. Although it may appear appropriate to purchase a twenty-megabyte hard disk—don't. For a few more dollars, you can obtain a forty-megabyte hard disk which should satisfy most of the needs of a small business. The information on the hard disk should be backed-up regularly on either floppy disks or tape. The next consideration is capacity and speed: 640K is generally sufficient RAM, but this will depend on the software. Ensure your computer can be upgraded to higher levels of RAM. A 12 to 15 megahertz (AT) is sufficient processing speed for most small-business operations; however, CAD/CAM systems will require the latest technology (i.e., 486, 586, N86) to run properly. You should be certain that the computer will allow appropriate peripherals, such as printers and modems.

The late 1980s saw the introduction of local area network systems (LAN). In this case, many—if not all—of the employees in the office, including you, will have a PC terminal which will be linked to a central "server" which will house the various computer programs and data being used for your company. The LAN systems allow each employee involved in the company's operation instantly to have access to the necessary information as he or she requires it. Our firm implemented a LAN system in 1989. All of the software packages being used by our staff for word processing, client financial statements, client monthly financial statements, corporate tax returns, personal tax returns, client T4s, client T5s, the Lotus 1-2-3 program for spreadsheet analysis, and so forth are housed in one central unit and our staff have access to these programs through the PC terminal at their desks.

As your business grows, you should consider establishing a local area network system (LAN) and engage the services of employees who are computer-oriented and are experienced with Word Perfect, Lotus 1-2-3, and the general applications of the standard programs. This will allow all employees to have first-hand contact with the necessary information required so they can perform their jobs efficiently.

The next step is to implement the various programs. We indicated the importance of planning earlier. Well, there is another important factor—patience. Determine your priorities for implementing the various programs. Don't try to run several programs simultaneously at the beginning. Introduce a new program only after the first one is working properly. In other words, introduce the accounts payable, accounts receivable, general ledger, and inventory-control modules one step at a time. Don't make the mistake of many impatient small-business owners who want to get the show on the road *now*. In some cases, it is appropriate to run a manual system parallel to the computer system. In a small business where the bookkeeper is probably only one person, it becomes a very time-consuming item to run two systems at one time. Slow and easy does it.

If the computer is replacing a manual bookkeeping system, then it is important that the manual bookkeeping system be working properly. The computer will not tidy up a sloppy manual system. In this case, you can expect total confusion in the initial stages and certainly a longer time before the system is running properly. Remember: your computer is not a magic wand.

The next step is to be certain that your personnel are trained on the computer. If your bookkeeper and other personnel are of the new computerized generation, then they will not be a problem. However, they will still have to be trained to use the specific programs. Employees who are not of the new computer generation will require more than a few days of training.

The long-term success of any small business's computer operation depends upon input from the owner. It is your company and your money. Consequently, don't leave the job of installing your first computer system to anyone but yourself. Granted, you may not be an expert, but you certainly have more interest than anyone else in seeing that the project is successful. To be successful, it requires your support and lots of "TLC."

One thing you can be sure of is that your first computer installation will be a traumatic experience. There is a saying in the computer industry that a poorly planned project takes three times as long to implement while a well-planned one takes only twice as long. You could be in for six months or even a year of trouble-shooting before all the bugs are out of the system.

13

STAYING IN BUSINESS

In the previous chapters, we dealt with buying yourself a
job. However, long-term success means staying in business.
  Statistics suggest that starting a small business is risky
business. The failure rate has been documented at four out
of five new firms within the first five years. However, a recent
study conducted in the United States by an official of the
U.S. Small Business Administration and a professor at the
Centre for Entrepreneurial Studies at Babson College indicates that the failure rate is 25% lower or three out of five
firms. In my view, that percentage is still pretty high.

Factors Contributing to Business Failure
Why do small businesses fail? Well, if you review the sum-
maries compiled by Dun & Bradstreet in *Classifications of
Causes of Business Failures in Canada*, you will notice that
97% revolve around some form of "poor management": lack
of experience in the specific industry or business, lack of
managerial experience, unbalanced experience, and incompetence. Dun & Bradstreet further classify 38% of the failures
as resulting from insufficient sales. This issue was addressed
in Chapters 8 and 11. It follows, then, that 62% of the failures
are the result of shortcomings in the other two legs of the
management tripod—operations and finance. I would like to
suggest that the majority of these failures are the result of
poor financial management. Financial management was dealt

with at some length in Chapters 9 and 10. A research study conducted by Ronald C. Clute, Professor of Accounting, University of Illinois, breaks down the causes of failure due to financial difficulty as follows: no or incomplete accounting records, 48%; poor or no inventory control, 39%; inadequate outside accountant, 18%; the other categories include problems in the area of cash flow and working capital analysis.

For the reader who has already bought his or her own job, I suggest that you reread Chapters 9 and 10. In my view, your company will never reach its optimum position unless the details of these chapters are carried out to the letter. Your outside accountant should be able to help you implement the systems and procedures. If your outside accountant is not available or is not interested in assisting you with assembling the monthly financial information that you need and implementing the inventory controls, then the accounting firm should be fired. In Chapter 7, we outlined how you might engage the services of a competent accounting firm that is interested in the well-being, profitability, and survival of your small business.

Remember that your accountant is your number one advisor. Without adequate support for your financial leg, your whole business will be wobbly. As suggested before, there are three types of small-business owners: the winners who will survive; the losers who will fall by the wayside in time; and, of course, the "living dead," who will flounder in good times and fail in bad times. The winners will have covered all the bases of the management tripod: marketing, operations, and finance. The winners will be good managers and make good decisions. They will gather the facts, measure the facts, and interpret the facts. They will not fly by the seat of their pants and make arbitrary decisions based on hearsay or how they feel at that particular moment of the day.

Stages and Cycles

Your new business will proceed through several stages.

1. The start-up stage, when you develop your idea, conduct some market research, determine the feasibility of the ven-

ture, prepare your business plan, and obtain the necessary financing.

2. The development stage, when you are in business selling your product and service, and eventually reach the break-even point.

3. The growth stage, when you begin to make a profit, hire additional staff, and improve profit. Up to this point, you will see an improvement in sales, an increase in personnel, increased activity, and your enthusiasm will be at an all-time high.

Like it or not, you will reach the fourth stage—consolidation. At this stage, sales level off, costs increase, and profits decrease. If your financial leg is wobbly and you do not have the information discussed in Chapter 10, then you may not realize that you have hit the consolidation stage until months later. For example, if you enter the consolidation stage in month six of year four, and you receive your financial statements for year four in the sixth month of year five, you won't necessarily recognize that you have entered a consolidation stage because there will only be a slight decline or leveling off of your profits. The profits in the first six months may offset the small decline in the latter six months. When you receive your annual financial statements for year five, in the sixth month of year six, you may have sustained lower profits or even losses for the full year that are possibly too late to recover. Without current accurate information (minimum monthly financial statements), you may believe that you have cash-flow problems and the bank doesn't really understand your company. The fact is you have entered the world of the loser or the living dead. You will probably be one of the 60% or 80% that fails in the first five years.

Other factors that you must consider are, for example, the economic environment and the long-term and short-term economic cycles. One of the classic theories of long-term cycles is referred to as the "long wave" or the "Kondratieff Wave." No one can really predict the future, but history, more often than not, repeats itself. An interesting trend over the past 200 years was documented by a Russian economist named

Kondratieff. Using statistics on prices, interest rates, and production, he discovered that there was roughly a fifty- to sixty-year business cycle. The first upward cycle, according to Kondratieff, began in the late 1780s. It reached a peak about 1815 and dropped to a trough about 1850. The second swing lasted into 1870 when the decline set in again. In simple terms, about every fifty to sixty years, the excesses of overheated growth are corrected by a deep depression. The roaring twenties, after World War I, was another peak that was followed by the Great Depression, which bottomed out in 1940. Followers of this theory traced the fourth peak to 1970.

According to this theory—remember that it's only a theory—the start of the secondary depression is in the 1980s. Unless we can come up with some new corrective measures and policies appropriate for our time, it will persist until the late 1990s.

I only mention this theory as something for anyone buying his or her own job to consider. The good news is that, if you realize what is going on around you, you can plan and make decisions accordingly. The advantage of being your own boss in your own business is that you will have more control over your own destiny. You will be able to deal with the effects of the long wave. Those working in big business or for someone else will find themselves in the hands of their bosses.

There are also short-term cycles. These are referred to as recessions. I am sure that many of you will remember the early 1980s when North America suffered one of the worst recessions in many years. In the initial months of the recession, companies that were poorly managed dropped by the wayside. I am informed that nine months into the recession many companies with heavy debts also fell by the wayside. The odds are that the first group of failures could be categorized as the losers and the living dead. However, the second group were probably better managed, but found themselves in an expansion position, over-levered, with heavy debt, and with a slight downturn in the economy, they were unable to service the debt load. So, the secret in turbulent times is maintain your flexibility as a small-business owner and maintain manageable debt. Remember that the only one who can really put you out of business is your banker when he or she calls your loan.

In 1989, some economists suggested that a recession is pending. Well, there are some similarities to the recession of 1981, in that recessions come in the form of the "inverted yield curve." Interest rates for investors normally vary in relation to the length of term for which the funds are committed: longer terms mean higher rates. The inverted yield curve means that the interest rate reduces in the longer term. When the economy is in a downturn, interest rates are generally lower. So the inverted yield curve suggests that if interest rates are lower in three to five years, then we can expect a downturn at that point. A one-year rate, for example, may be 11%, but in three years, it may decrease to 10.75% or lower. This suggests a higher demand for money in the short term as opposed to the long term and signals tight money times, say, by the 1990s.

Reading the Signals

In my view, true entrepreneurs (people in effective control of commercial undertakings) will survive both the long- and short-wave cycles. They will manage the balance sheet. Some of the early warning signals of troubled times ahead can be obtained by simply calculating key ratios on a monthly basis and monitoring the trends. The most significant key ratio is the current ratio (current assets divided by current liabilities), because it measures the liquidity of your business. (See Chapter 10.) As we pointed out earlier, the higher this ratio is, the better. If your current ratio is running at about 2:1 and decreases to 1.6:1 and then to 1.3:1, you know that your liquidity is shrinking and that you could be headed for a financial crisis. The next key ratio is the debt-to-equity ratio (total liabilities divided by shareholders' equity). The lower it is, the better. If the monthly calculation of this ratio indicates a trend upward, say, from 2:1 to 2.5:1 to 3:1, then your company is heading to an over-levered position, which suggests high risk and is a warning bell for your banker. Your banker is very conscious of your current ratio and your debt-to-equity ratio. Any negative trends can indicate a pending financial crisis.

Other warning signals can be determined by calculating, on a monthly basis, the accounts receivable turnover (annualized sales divided by accounts receivable balance). The higher it is the better. The gross profit return on inventory or GPROI is also important (annualized gross profit divided by inventory times 100). The higher it is, the better. If the monthly accounts receivable turnover is trending downward, this means that your customers are slowing their payments to you, perhaps because they are in a cash bind themselves. These customers may have difficulty paying their bills in the future. Don't allow more than ten percent of your accounts receivable to be in the hands of any one customer and don't allow your bigger clients to push you around and drag out their accounts receivable because they are "good customers." Turbulent times require guts management.

If the GPROI is trending downward from, say, 250% to 225% to 200%, you can be sure that you have too much of the wrong inventory. The bank will only finance 25% to 50% of it, and you may be stuck with some obsolete stock.

To monitor the inventory, you should make certain to prepare the gross profit and inventory analysis set out in Chapter 10. This will allow you to zero in on the areas and the specific products where the GPROI is decreasing. Obviously, if you have a point-of-sale computer for a retail operation, the details should be available from the various printouts.

Nonfinancial Causes of Business Failure

The above section sets out the financial reasons for small-business failures. However, there are some other reasons. One of these is boredom. Some small-business owners, having survived the development and growth stages and having come to be considered successful, get bored. This is referred to as the comfort stage. In many cases, owners feel that their earlier anxieties and fears of failure are well behind them. Additional staff is hired to handle many of the tasks previously performed by the owner, while he or she is making a good buck and enjoying the good life.

If you have survived all of these stages, including the consolidation stage, then what can go wrong? As your enthusiasm wanes and you find yourself involved in pet projects from which you derive personal pleasure, you will have effectively left the helm of the once prime object of your life, your own business. An example of this is the small-business owner who was in his own business for about twenty years. The company was profitable, earning between $100,000 to $150,000 a year. The owner hired an inexperienced college grad to manage the company, so that he could do his own thing. It was not long after that the receiver showed up.

Another small-business owner got bored and devoted his time to a pet project and used the "cash cow" for financing. You guessed it: receivership. As long as you own your own business, *you cannot abdicate responsibility of the ultimate management.*

I also believe in the personal five-year cycle. Whether you are in your own business or working for another company, there must be some change or modification in your work activity every five years. If not, you will get bored. Therefore, you should look to other areas in your company where you might be involved or take on additional lines, or expand in order to alter your personal job slightly. If you find that this is impossible, do one of two things: sell the business or hire a good, experienced manager. But when you hire a good manager, you still cannot abdicate total responsibility for your business. You must continue to operate in the same manner by obtaining the financial information set out in Chapter 10 and meeting at least monthly with the manager to review performance and compare it against projections set out in the business plan.

Another reason for failure has to do with the personal financial affairs of the small-business owner. Too many small-business owners confuse the finances of the business with personal finances. We performed a receivership in the mid-1980s where a company had been earning over $150,000 per year. However, the owner in an effort to "keep up with the Joneses" bought a $450,000 home, sold his current home for $150,000, and took on a $300,000 mortgage. The cost of servicing this mortgage together with new furniture, drapes, and so forth for the new home required advances over and above the normal salary to finance. The business owner did not realize the extent of the after-tax cost until the accountants arrived at year-end. He had drawn $50,000 from the company to satisfy these expenses. At the time, his personal income tax rate was fifty percent. This means that the pre-tax cost to the company was $100,000 ($50,000 advance plus $50,000 income tax). The year-end adjustment to the financial statements of double the amount of draw resulted in a loss to the company for that year. The drain of cash led to eventual receivership: the loss of both the business and the home. Chapter 14 will deal with personal financial planning and some general personal organization for small-business owners.

Another item that can pose major problems for the continuation of your small business is internal and external theft. Almost weekly, you will see articles in the newspaper such as "Employee, 29, swindled firm out of $98,000." "Company inertia, ineptitude contribute to employee theft." "Retailers losing billions from shoplifting, staff theft." A survey conducted by an international consulting firm suggests that "sticky fingers and slipshod tracking of merchandise are costing retailers billions of dollars in the United States." According to the survey, apprehended thieves are 89% customers and 11% employees. A publication of the Retail Council of Canada *1989 Shrinkage Survey of Canadian Retailers* suggests that shrinkage is attributable to all sources and amounts to a low of .003 percent of sales up to a horrifying high of 10%. The report indicates that the retailers included in the survey suggest that over half of the shrinkage is attributable to shoplifting by customers, about one quarter of the loss is estimated to be theft by employees, and the remainder—under 20%—is bookkeeping and paperwork errors.

You may be quick to suggest that your employees are truly honest people. Well, you are probably right. However, it is your responsibility as the business owner to establish the proper controls to protect your employees from themselves. The main reason employees are honest is the fear of being caught. If adequate operational controls are in place, with no loopholes, then the honest employee will not falter from the straight course (See Chapter 9.)

Some of you may suggest that your accountant or auditor will protect you from these problems. Well, this could not be further from the truth. The majority of small-business companies do not have audited annual financial statements. However, even audited financial statements will not necessarily detect any fraud. The auditor, of course, will review the procedures and controls and make recommendations for improvements, but the act of auditing will not necessarily catch any fraudulent employee.

Shoplifting appears to be at monumental levels for retailers. It is, therefore, important that any retailer establish the physical controls necessary for protection. One control is the alarm system that can be used by retailers whereby they attach a tag to the merchandise that can only be removed by the cashier. If the item is taken from the store without the cashier removing this tag, then the alarm is set off at the doorway.

Physical control also means that high-risk products are placed in an area closely supervised by employees.

This further emphasizes the need to review Chapter 9 and implement the operational control systems to protect your employees from themselves. Another suggestion is to have your accountants, who normally do a review of your annual financial statements, perform a management audit. This means they will review all of the procedures and controls in your company and make the recommendations necessary to plug any loopholes. And, remember, it is your responsibility to keep your employees honest.

Several years ago, we were approached by an individual who had started a small contracting firm several months earlier. There were no financial reports, and he received no information other than to get phone calls from the bank to discuss overdrafts. This trusting individual had an "honest" bookkeeper looking after the firm and the paperwork. On reviewing his operation, we discovered that over $30,000 in cheques had been written and cashed by the bookkeeper. This was the proverbial straw that broke the camel's back, and the small-business owner found himself out of business. He had also lost the financing required to buy another job.

Another reason some companies fail to stay in business is a bad partnership. In my view, partnerships are probably the best way to go in terms of resolving the problems you might have with your management tripod (marketing, operations, and finance). One or more partners, who can complement your skills and experience, will contribute tremendously to the long-term success of the company. The other advantage of partners is you have someone to talk to, whom you respect. Decisions can be made that will cover all of the bases. In my view, this will minimize major mistakes, of which it can take only one to spell the death knell for any small business. The secret, of course, is to get the right partner or partners. On reviewing our clientele, we see the good news and bad news. In many cases, partnerships have been long-term and have proven to be very successful. However, some have encountered serious problems and some have broken up. The breakup of a partnership can be as traumatic as the breakup of marriage. The main difference is that, in the business partnership breakup, the business itself may disappear.

A few years ago, we were called in by a bank to assist two partners who were at loggerheads. In this case, one partner was managing the plant and the other was managing the front office and the marketing. This was a good combination. For several years, they had earned good profits, were both driving big cars, and were truly successful small-business owners.

These two partners had reached the point where they had lost trust and faith in each other and had decided to split. Our job was to provide them with a reasonable valuation of the shares and to help negotiate a reasonable settlement for both sides. Our valuation of the shares was something in the area of $600,000. As usual, both parties felt that we had undervalued the shares. Surprisingly, this included the party who wished to purchase. In the first instance, the partner in the plant was to buy out the partner in the front office, who was about twenty years older. For some reason, this reversed itself, and the front-office partner paid something in the area of $375,000 for his other partner's shares (at least $75,000 too much). Within six months, the company was in receivership because it was saddled with the onerous debt incurred on redemption of the partner's shares. The front-office partner was not able to manage the plant properly.

These partners had no agreement. If you are contemplating partnership with anyone, it is important before you commence the business to have your lawyer draw up a reasonable partnership agreement so that you will have some basis of termination in the event that the partnership does not work out. Ideally, the shotgun approach is the best. In this case, one partner offers to purchase the other partner's shares for a certain price, and the offeree has the option to accept or to buy out the offering partner's shares for the same price. This keeps everyone honest. However, in some cases, where one of the partners has substantially more assets than the other, such an agreement is hardly fair, since that partner could make an unfair offer that could not be taken up by the financially weaker partner. In this case, some method of valuing the shares of the company must be included in the shareholders' agreement.

Another way to terminate your role as an entrepreneur is to expand too quickly. The message is: Planned growth. When I discussed cash management in Chapter 10, I referred to the client who wished to increase sales by $40,000 per month and discovered that the increase in accounts receivable and inventory would be much higher than the initial profits derived from the expansion. Here is another example. Back in the mid-1970s, my company was involved with a thriving retailer who was making exceptionally good profits in one store. We got involved just after he opened his third store. His whole focus was on profits, with no consideration given to cash flow. The cash cow—the first store—was used to finance both the second and third store openings. The profits in the second and third stores did not materialize as quickly as estimated. These stores were opened within a year of each other, and the ultimate effect was that the cash cow could no longer finance the two losers. The company found itself in the hands of the receiver.

A reasonable approach would be to set up the second store with proper financing for that store without dipping into the pockets of the cash cow. Certainly, the cash cow could be used as collateral in financing for the banker, but the actual financing for inventory, fixtures, and initial operating losses should be covered with outside financing. Also, if more than one store is planned, future stores should be opened every two or three years, not two in one year. The message here is don't let your greed for profits blind you to the necessity of cash flow. Don't forget the balance sheet.

I am sure there are other reasons for not staying in business and being your own boss, but the major ones are set out above. The key item to remember is that the bank is the only one that can really put you out of business. Maintain a manageable bank debt in both good and bad times.

Surviving the Downturns

Let's look at what you might do if you find yourself in a cash bind or a period of consolidation. You can be sure of one thing: "The buck starts with you." Although it may be difficult to admit, you are probably the reason for the problems. You may blame other things, such as high interest rates, the general economy, the recession, or whatever, but a true entrepreneur would have "control." He or she would be looking ahead and moving with the times. Remember that your major asset is flexibility. You can make decisions and put them into action the same day. Spearheading a turnaround will test your leadership ability and your ability to be a "guts" manager.

To survive, you must fight two battles at the same time. First and foremost, the balance sheet must be put in order. Second, if your income statement suggests you are losing money, you must stop the hemorrhaging. To check on the balance sheet, you must review your key ratios.

You should strive to minimize your assets and maximize liabilities (including shareholders' equity). Simultaneously, you must take a hard look at your income statement. The positive approach, of course, is to improve the sales of your higher-profit items. On the other hand, if you are in a downturn position, the odds are that this positive approach may not be the short-term answer. Remember that to be in business for the long term, you must be in business for the short term. Survival thinking must be short term.

If your investigation shows that the accounts receivable turnover is decreasing, specific action should be taken immediately to collect on the older accounts. In addition, it might be possible to collect on the current accounts of bigger customers by offering incentive for immediate payment. I can speak first hand to this. Before starting my own business, I was involved with a company that was in a downturn position. We were required to pay our suppliers before receiving product for delivery to our customers. This meant calling our good customers and offering a 5% cash discount in return for immediate payment. We had to persist with this approach for about five months before we were able to loosen our cash bind. This increased our finance costs and decreased our profit, but it improved our balance sheet and was the key to our short-term survival.

The next step is to review the GPROI calculations. If the GPROI has been decreasing, you have too much slow-moving inventory. This means you must review the inventory on hand, sell off all slow-moving or obsolete inventory at virtually any price (forget profits), and get the cash in.

Review fixed assets for possible sale and leaseback or outright sale and rent new equipment for the short-term future.

Review accounts payable and attempt to arrange longer terms with suppliers. The odds are this will be a problem in your present financial condition, so you will be required to lean on your suppliers. It is critical, when you find yourself in this position, to observe one rule: Do not lie. You are much better off paying $100 on a regular basis to show good faith than suggesting that the "cheque is in the mail." If your suppliers lose faith in your integrity or honesty, you are doomed. Earlier, I suggested that only your banker could put you out of business. Well, that isn't quite true. A major supplier can issue a writ and place you in bankruptcy. But this is not too common. Usually, there won't be enough money to pay off secured creditors (your bank), the trustee, let alone any unsecured creditors.

You must also take a hard look at your operating expenses with a view to minimizing them. In the short term, it may be necessary to lay off some employees even if you consider them key to the long-term profitability of your company. Your plan of action must be prepared immediately to determine who specifically should be laid off and the dollar savings involved. Generally, there is not much you can do in the short run with occupancy costs unless, of course, your lease is month to month or is up for renewal shortly. If your occupancy cost is in excess of 10% of gross profit then you should move to less costly facilities. Other expenses should be reviewed in detail and virtually no commitment should be made for any expenses unless it is absolutely necessary to the short-term survival of the business. For example, you may still require postage, and gas and oil for vehicles, but you don't need new stationery or expensive advertising.

Once you have reviewed the balance sheet and the income statement and decided upon a basic strategy for improving the cash position and profits, write that strategy down. Establish a time frame for each item: accounts receivables will be in line by a certain date, inventory by a certain date, fixed assets sold by a certain date, and so forth.

Once the plan is established, the next step is to phone your banker. Strange as it might seem, he or she will be your best ally during these difficult times. You need his or her support. However, that support will not be forthcoming if you are not willing to grab the bull by the horns and establish a plan of action to bring your balance sheet and income statement into line.

In the meantime, you should consider alternative financing sources. This can include so-called "love money" from friends or relatives, remortgaging your home if there is any money available for financing, or possibly selling your home and moving into rented facilities as a *temporary* measure. You will no doubt find at this time that the banker is a little edgy and will certainly not wish to increase your line of credit. It is also not a very good time to attempt to change banks, as you can be sure that other bankers will be aware of your financial problems.

As a last resort, you may consider "factoring" your accounts receivable. Factoring means that you sell the good accounts receivable to a financial institution for the face value less a discounted amount and pay interest on the amounts until these are collected by the factoring company. A major problem is that once you decide to discontinue factoring your accounts receivable, you will have anywhere from two to six weeks without cash flow. In the mid-1970s we got involved with a company that had just gone through a major turnaround and had used a factoring company to assist in this program. Obviously, this factoring worked as the company was still in business. In the next twelve months, the owners of the business found themselves in dire financial straits in an effort to increase profits as well as pay their bills. By having monthly financial reports and up-to-date financial information on receivables, inventory, and other aspects of their business, this company successfully bridged the gap.

I would hope that anyone who reads the previous chapters in this book would not find it necessary to read this chapter. If you implement all of the systems, procedures, and management tips set out in the previous chapters, you will not enter a downturn cycle and will not be required to perform the heart-rending gutsy management process that I have just discussed.

14

PERSONAL FINANCIAL PLANNING

Two Businesses: The Company Business and the Personal Business

Now that you have bought your job and you are your own boss, you must recognize that you are now in two businesses: your small-business business and your personal business. It is a mistake to consider the funds in your business as your own. When you obtained the necessary financing to start up or purchase a business, the financing was put in place for that purpose. The plan also included your remuneration.

You are better to think of yourself as an employee and to treat yourself as such. Granted, you have scrimped and saved during the early years and probably deserve to reap some of the rewards of your personal and family sacrifices. You may feel that the improved profits and growth of your new business suggest that you deserve a bigger home, faster car, and longer vacations. Quite frankly, I agree.

However, before embarking on this improved personal life-style, it is necessary that you perform the detailed planning that will satisfy these personal goals. They must be compatible with your business goals. The same ingredients that go into making the company a success need to be applied personally as well. As a successful business owner, you prepare monthly forecasts of income and expenses and follow up with monthly financial reports to monitor the plan. You make sure that you are on track and, if not, you are able to do something about it immediately.

Well, the same basic management technique applies to your personal business. There is an old expression: Failing to plan is planning to fail. When you apply this adage to your personal affairs, it translates into worrisome bills which require payment through the cash cow—your company—and can result in the downfall of your business.

Newly successful business owners are ripe targets. They are reaching the top of their growth stage where the profits are increasing and the cash flow has leveled off. It is so easy to take out an extra $1,000 or $500 to cover some personal expenses. Costs, however, will be much higher when the accountant does your year-end tally. Many business owners find themselves with large shareholder advances that must be repaid to the company. This is a double whammy. The advances will increase the personal income-tax liability of the small-business owner. For example, if you are in the 44% marginal rate and you draw out $30,000 from the business for personal use, you are actually depriving the company of $54,000 before taxes. You have incurred a tax liability of about $24,000. In other words, when the year-end statements for your company are finalized, a journal entry will be prepared which will be a debit, or a charge, to expenses of about $54,000 (a credit to your advance account of $30,000 and a credit to income taxes payable of $24,000). Therefore, if you felt that your company was in a position to earn $100,000 for that year, then you have just eliminated $54,000 of that and ended up with only $46,000 profit before corporate income taxes.

In Chapter 13, I outlined the failure of one successful small-business owner who wanted to keep up with the Joneses when he bought his dream home. The money required to pay for the high mortgage, redecorating, and landscaping was withdrawn from the company before payment of any personal income taxes. At that time, his personal income tax rate was fifty percent. So, the additional liability for personal income tax was the same amount. Any financial statements up to that point would not reflect the additional charge against the profits for the draw and the income tax liability.

Then there is the individual in the small service company who did not put himself on salary, but took ad hoc payments as required. With the stroke of a pen he was able to write himself cheques in various amounts—$500, $1,000—whatever he needed. The bank called us in to review the financial affairs of this company (which by the way had no monthly financial reports), and I was quick to discover that although the company had earned something in the area of $30,000 before the owner's remuneration, the draw up to that point was $60,000 and this attracted an additional $30,000 tax liability. The operating loss after recording these details was $60,000 ($30,000 profit less draw and income tax liability of $90,000).

Clearly, personal financial planning by all business owners is extremely important, not only for the business but for the personal lifestyle of the owner and his or her family.

I would like to suggest that you should operate your personal business in the same manner as you operate your small business. Prepare a personal plan or budget and then monitor it on a monthly basis to see that you are on track. Unfortunately, too many people, including business owners have no idea where the money really goes. I can speak first hand to this. Prior to taking on partners in our firm, I was a sole owner and did exactly what I am telling you not to do. I did not put myself on a regular salary or draw. I did not have a personal budget and I took money from the business to satisfy what I thought were my needs, but in many cases were just my wants. As it turns out, my withdrawals did not cause any financial hardship to the company because I was able to pay my income taxes as I went and, of course, the lump sum at year-end for those ad hoc withdrawals. However, when I prepared my income tax return, I discovered that my personal taxable earnings were substantially higher than I felt reasonable. Big question: Where did the money go?

I performed a simple exercise which I suggest everyone should do. I reviewed my chequebook for the previous calendar year and was able to segregate my spending into four general categories: 1. regular monthly items, such as mortgage, telephone, and groceries; 2. irregular items, which fell into various months, such as property taxes, insurance, clothing, and gifts; 3. unexpected expenses such as car or home repairs, and 4. big-event items such as vacations and home furnishings.

The most difficult item to assess was my "walkaround"

money that went for lunches, haircuts, entertainment, and whatever. Now that I knew where the money went, it was a case of determining what I should be spending in the various categories of expenses. This was to be my personal business plan. In discussions with my wife, we arrived at what we considered reasonable amounts in the various categories, added them up, estimated what the income tax would be, and that became my salary before taxes. I then set up a little spreadsheet for six months showing columns for forecast and actual for each month and down the left side listed the various types of expenditures. To this day, I prepare my annual plan and I monitor it on a monthly basis.

I suggest that there are many approaches to personal planning, but the above is very simple and it takes me about one-half hour at the year-end and about five minutes a month to summarize the details.

Every small-business owner should perform the same simple task, establish priorities of where the money should go, and prepare an annual personal business plan to be monitored on a monthly basis. It sounds simple and it is. One of the by-products is the elimination of the problem of not knowing where the money goes. You will have controls—and be a personal entrepreneur. This approach will go a long way to relieving the stress associated with running a small business, and it is critical in helping you attain your personal financial goals.

Tax Savings for Small-Business Owners

Now that your personal financial house is in order, it is time to consider short- and long-term personal financial planning. The secret to remember in any planning is to minimize your after-tax expenses and defer income taxes. Your major expenses include the mortage on your home, your automobile, medical and dental bills and, of course, personal expenses for clothing, groceries, entertainment, and so forth.

As a business owner, you are also your own employee. And you can bestow benefits on that employee that can minimize income taxes. One example involves the purchase of your home: the mortgage can be held by your company (assuming the funds are available). For example, if you personally hold a $100,000 mortgage at 12%, you are paying $12,000 interest per year in after-tax dollars. If you are in the 44% tax bracket, you are in effect removing over $21,000 from the company's earnings, paying the tax, and using the remainder to pay the interest on the mortgage. If when you purchase your home, you borrowed the money from the company as suggested above, then you can receive an interest-free loan. This means you will not have to remove $21,000 from the company's profits in order to satisfy the mortgage interest payments. However, there is a cost. The government suggests that this is a personal benefit to you as an employee of the company. The amount of the personal benefit is termed "imputed interest." In other words, the government sets a rate of interest on the mortgage held by your company and this amount is added to your T4 as an employee benefit and you pay personal taxes on the amount of the interest. The rate varies, but is generally lower than what you might be paying personally. For example, if the standard is, say, 12%, then the imputed interest may be running about 11%. In the above case, 11% or $11,000 would be added to your T4, on which you would pay tax. If you are at the 44% tax level, then your tax cost in after-tax dollars would be $4,840, as opposed to $12,000. Normally, in this case, you would only be required to take out from the company before tax about $8,600 in order to pay for the mortgage finance costs. In other words, the pre-tax cost to the company would be reduced from $21,000 to about $8,600. Granted, you would have to repay the mortgage over a reasonable period of time, but then this is a requirement that you have anyway with a third-party mortgage.

Another advantage as an owner-employee is the manner in which you can deal with your car expenses. The income tax reform initiated by Finance Minister, Michael Wilson, has muddied the waters in this area. Consequently, you should discuss the details of this with your tax accountant before proceeding with owning and having a company car or taking car allowances.

Your health and dental after-tax costs can be virtually eliminated by establishing a group insurance plan to cover these expenses. There are generally two types of dental plans.

One might be considered the basic plan and the other the superior plan. The basic plan covers normal dental care whereas the superior plan will cover cosmetic dental care. The premium is tax deductible by your company.

Income splitting with family members becomes another method of optimizing your after-tax remuneration. The Canadian personal income tax system has three levels of taxation which were effective on January 1, 1988: 17% on taxable income up to $27,500; 26% on taxable income between $27,501 and $55,000; and 29% on taxable income over $55,000. To this must be added the respective provincial personal income tax. If your spouse or dependents are contributing to the operation of your company, then remuneration paid to them for their personal use will probably be taxed at the lowest rate of 17% plus the provincial taxes. This is certainly lower than your probable tax rate of 29%.

Rather than receiving the total personal income and distributing it back to your spouse and dependents, you are much further ahead to pay them at the 17% rate. The examples I am using in the tax planning areas assumes the high federal tax rate of 29% plus 52% for the province (29% plus 52% of 29% equals 44%). This will vary by province. If the spouse was included as part of the structuring of the share capital of the company, then about $24,000 of dividends can flow to him or her tax free, provided he or she has no other personal taxable income. In addition, of course, children can be paid at a reasonable level for efforts put into your company's operation. These funds can be used for the purchase of personal clothing and school expenses which are normally after-tax expenses to you.

In some cases, a "family trust" is appropriate for the distribution of funds to children who are not involved in the operation of the company, in which case no salary or compensation would be deemed reasonable.

If you happen to be a member of a sports or social club and if that membership can reasonably be viewed as contributing to the promotion of your business, then membership fees should be paid by your company. For example, if the annual membership fee is $1,000 and if you are in the 44% tax bracket, you will be using about $1,800 in pre-tax earnings to pay the fee. If the company pays the fee, only $1,000 is required. Although the amount is not deductible for tax purposes, it is still far better for the company to pay in after-tax dollars (equivalent to $1,282 before income tax) than for you to pay in after-tax dollars (equivalent to $1,800).

As a small-business owner, you cannot afford to make any major decision that affects taxation (including paying yourself) without conferring with a tax expert. As I mentioned before, all accountants may be perceived as tax specialists, but only a very few can be considered true experts. And tax planning is critical for any business owner, precisely because the interconnection between the company and personal business must be dealt with effectively. Appropriate tax planning must take place in order for you to optimize your after-tax position.

Too many small-business owners believe that reducing taxes constitutes the main thrust of tax planning. This couldn't be further from the truth. The main thrust is to optimize your after-tax income. We have numerous examples of clients who have saved on taxes by purchasing MURBs, limited partnerships, and some exotic mining and oil tax plans. But in addition to reducing taxes, such investments minimized their after-tax income.

You will hear many of your colleagues expounding on how they saved taxes. Your response should be: "What did it cost you?" The following is an example of what can happen. A mining conglomerate offered the sale of shares of various mines for $50,000. In the first year, the taxes returned to the purchaser through investment-tax credits and so forth was $35,000. The saving of $35,000 in taxes can be considered a great move. However, there was a net of $15,000 invested in this group of mining companies. Were they worth $15,000? In one case, our client indicated that they weren't. So why would you spend $50,000 to save $35,000? There are numerous examples of tax savings that create negative cash flows for small-business owners over future years.

There is an old expression: "A penny saved is a penny earned." In personal and tax planning, a penny saved is almost two pennies earned.

With personal business planning, it should be possible to

make funds available for investment purposes. I suggest that excess cash that might be available in the business should be distributed either to you personally or to a holding company. The alternative to this is to leave the funds in the company and to make short-term investments to optimize the use of the funds. The problem is that, if you wish in the future to sell the shares of your company to make use of the $500,000 tax-free capital gain, these funds will probably have to be distributed at that time and may attract substantial personal income taxes. If these funds are distributed to you personally in the form of dividends, then the ultimate personal and corporate tax will be the same as if you had taken a salary. However, if you form a holding company to hold the shares of the operating business, then the dividends issued to the holding company will be tax free. In other words, the only income taxes that will be paid on the profits of the operating company will be by the operating company at 22% of these taxable profits. Therefore, the holding company can receive up to $.78 of every $1.00 earned by the operating company. If you receive the profits personally, then the effective corporate and personal tax has an effective top marginal rate of about 44%.

But before you jump into forming a holding company, you should discuss the details with your tax accountant to be certain this move is the right one for you at this time. You should realize that once the shares are rolled into the holding company, the operating company's shares are no longer eligible for the $500,000 tax-free capital gain. However, you can sell the shares of the holding company to take advantage of the tax-free capital gain. But in the future you will probably have many personal assets in the holding company that would have to be distributed before the sale. It is possible, in some cases, that the cost will offset any savings on selling shares.

Planning for Retirement

The main reason for personal and tax planning is to enable business owners to enjoy the lifestyle of their choice—in other words, to have control over the funds they earn in order to do the things they wish. However, in the long term, such planning is also critical for retirement. It is important to be able to retire and live in the style to which you have become accustomed. Unfortunately, too many don't consider retirement planning until they are over fifty. In some cases, this can be too late.

Exhibit 18 sets out the effect of inflation at 5%, at 7½%, and 10%. In 1990, the inflation rate was hovering in the 5% area. Let's look at the implications of inflation for an individual who is 40 years old, plans to retire at 65, and currently requires $100,000 of pre-tax income to maintain his or her lifestyle. At age 65, 25 years later, assuming a 5% inflation rate throughout that period, he or she will need a pre-tax annual income of $338,600 ($100,000 times 3.386) to maintain the same lifestyle. Later on in this chapter, we will see why the amount needn't be quite this high. Current annuity tables suggest that you will receive about $12,000 per year for every $100,000 available for purchase of an annuity. In this case, the individual will require about $2,800,000 in order to receive $338,600 per year ($338,600 divided by $12,000 times $100,000). Pretty scary, isn't it?

EXHIBIT 18

INFLATION
$1.00

Year	5%	7-1/2%	10%
1	1.050	1.075	1.100
5	1.276	1.435	1.610
10	1.629	2.061	2.593
15	2.079	2.958	4.177
20	2.653	4.247	6.727
25	3.386	6.098	10.834

God help us if inflation is at 7½% or 10%, in which case the amount required to sustain the current lifestyle would be $5,000,000 or $9,000,000 respectively. With the increase in lifespan, we can all expect to live to be 80 or more. Although our financial needs tend to diminish in the latter years, no one wants to look forward to financial hardship between the ages of 65 and 75. As Harold Taylor once said: "It is all very well to say eat, drink and be merry, for tomorrow we may die—but what if you run out of money before you run out of life?" So, plan early.

Registered Retirement Savings Plans

How do you increase your personal wealth in order to maintain your lifestyle on retirement? Well, the best approach is to contribute the maximum to a Registered Retirement Savings Plan (RRSP). Exhibit 19 sets out a comparison of an investment of $1,000 per year with a 12% return in an RRSP and the same investment outside an RRSP. In 1990, you can invest the lesser of 20% of your income for calendar year 1990 or $7,500. The deduction limit for 1991 is changed to the lesser of 18% of your earned income for 1990 to a maximum of $11,500. The maximum contribution for the years 1992 through 1995 are 18% of the previous year's earned income to a maximum of $12,500, $13,500, $14,500, and $15,500 respectively. In 25 years, the annual investment of $1,000 at 12% compounds to $149,333 in an RRSP and, because of tax on interest income, to only $29,078 outside the RRSP. Thus, with an RRSP, you are deferring income tax on the monies invested, together with the monies earned until such time as they are taken out at retirement. This is the best tax deferment. It is possible that your maximum rate on retirement may be less than the current rate. That's direct savings. You can be sure of one thing, however. You will be paying it in dollars that, 25 years from now at 5% inflation, will be worth about one-third of current dollars.

If you purchased a home before you started your business and were unable to put the mortgage through the company, then you will have a mortgage upon which you are paying interest in after-tax dollars. This mortgage should be paid off as quickly as possible. Consequently, on the one hand, I am suggesting that you should pay down this after-tax cost as soon as possible and, on the other hand, that you should put as much as possible into your RRSP. If you are short

EXHIBIT 19

RETURN ON RRSP INVESTMENT

Assume:
1. $1,000 invested in RRSP
2. 12% return

End of Year	In an RRSP	Outside an RRSP
1	$ 1,120	$ 530
5	7,115	2,987
10	19,654	6,985
15	41,753	12,753
20	80,698	19,496
25	149,333	29,078

of money, you have a decision to make. Should you take any available funds to pay off the mortgage or should you put them into an RRSP? As a general statement, I would recommend that you pay down the mortgage and when this is completed, start investing in an RRSP. However, there is no hard-and-fast rule. I suggest that you consult a tax expert who can point out the specific dollar advantages of both approaches.

Another item to consider when contributing to your RRSP is the timing. For example, for any tax year, you can contribute these funds from January of that year to March 1 of the following year. All too often, people tend to wait until the last minute and contribute during January to March 1 of the following year. You should realize that contributing in January of the current year instead of twelve to fourteen months later will result in about an 11% increase in your RRSP funds. Therefore, consider contributing at the earliest possible time.

If your spouse has no taxable income, then you should establish a spousal RRSP. You are, in fact, setting up a second RRSP fund, but in your spouse's name. The maximum annual contribution remains the same as indicated previously in this chapter. But the amounts can be split between your RRSP and your spouse's RRSP. This means that the funds that you would be contributing to your own plan can be contributed in your spouse's name. This is a means of income splitting at retirement. The optimum tax planning is to have the RRSP funds equal for each spouse. This will minimize income tax payments during retirement.

It is sometimes a good idea to establish a self-administered RRSP. This means that the funds are held in trust by a stockbroker or a trust company and you can dictate the method or the means of investment for your fund. However, not all investments qualify for an RRSP. Generally speaking, all securities registered in the major Canadian stock exchanges, T-Bills, government bonds, qualified mortgages, mutual funds, and essentially normal securities qualify. Items such as exotic metals, gold, silver, and so forth do not qualify. Also, if you are willing to go through the paperwork, you can pay off the existing mortgage on your home through a self-administered RRSP and make interest payments to your own RRSP fund. Not too many individuals have taken advantage of this because of the trust-company fees and the paperwork involved. Quite frankly, the only advantage is that you can give yourself an open mortgage that can be paid off at any time. By the way, the rate of interest must be competitive with the market. In some cases, this can be higher than any return you might get from any other investments you make.

Return on Investment and Return of Investment
In choosing your investments, you should be aware of the following basic law of investment: return on investment (ROI) varies directly with the risk and inversely with the liquidity of the investment. In other words, risk and reward go hand in hand: the higher the reward, the higher the risk. Likewise, the higher the liquidity, the lower the return. For example, an investment in real estate is considered high risk and low liquidity and, therefore, warrants a higher return, whereas an investment in Government of Canada bonds is low risk, high liquidity and, therefore, gets a low return.

The basis, then, upon which to establish an investment portfolio within or outside of your self-administered RRSP is to establish your return-on-investment goals. If you can live happily with a 10% per annum return on your investment, then you can attain this at the present time with very low risk and very high liquid investments. However, if you are looking for a 20% return, then your funds will have to be invested in higher-risk and lower-liquidity items. Possibly a mixture of low-risk and high-risk investments should be considered. Again, everyone is different, everyone has his or her own personal goals, so everyone will have a different plan. Exhibit 20 sets out the results of an RRSP contribution at $5,500 per year with return on investment at 8%, 12%, 16%, and 20%. You will notice that after 35 years at 12%, the fund should be $2,659,000. However, at 16%, the fund is nearly triple at $7,150,000.

As I noted, ROI means return on investment. All too often, individuals get carried away by hoping to exploit and increase the ROI to above-normal levels. Well, when it comes to personal financial planning, ROI means something just a little different. Return *of* investment is far more important than return on investment. The higher the return on investment, the higher the risk and the possibility of a lack of return of investment. Always remember that you are gambling with your own future.

EXHIBIT 20

RISK AND REWARD
RRSP CONTRIBUTION — $5,500 PER YEAR
($000's omitted)

Years	8%	12%	16%	20%
10	86	108	136	171
20	272	444	736	1,232
30	673	1,487	3,383	7,800
35	1,024	2,659	7,150	19,459

How to Approach Retirement Planning

The question, then, is *how* to plan for a retirement that protects your current lifestyle. The first thing to do is summarize your expenses, as set out above. The next is to adjust these expenses to reflect what they will be when you retire. For example, if there is a mortgage on your home, it will no doubt be paid off, and you can eliminate that expense. Your children's school expenses will no longer apply. Vacation expenses, however, will probably increase. Clothing costs will no doubt decrease, and so forth. You can then determine the adjusted after-tax amount that you and your spouse will require annually through your retirement. You must also make a list of your assets and your liabilities in order to determine your current net worth. It is now time to make some assumptions. For example, what inflation rate do you expect to be in place between now and the date of retirement? What amounts of investment will you be placing in your RRSP and outside the RRSP between now and retirement? What rates of return are you targeting: for example, 10% or 12%? At this point, your accountant, by using some of the normal spreadsheet computer programs, can calculate what the accumulated investments in and out of your RRSP would amount to at the time of retirement, as well as what your current retirement costs would be at the time of retirement including inflation. By using a factor of, say, $12,000 per $100,000 of investment, you can calculate whether you would have enough funds available at your retirement date. This calculation should not include your home or your business. If there is a shortfall in the RRSPs and other investments, then the value of your home and business should make up the shortfall. If there is a major shortfall, then planning must be done now to increase the contributions to your RRSP and increase outside investments. It is not a good idea to revise your return-on-investment goals from, say, 12% to 15% or 20%. You could put your total investment portfolio at risk in an attempt to get the higher reward.

This may all sound very complicated. However, there are people who can help. There are financial planners available who can assist you in developing your retirement plan. They can also recommend the various types of investments to meet your personal goals. One caution about these planners is that some of them are selling product. In other words, a stock-broker is selling stocks, an insurance broker is selling insurance, and a mutual-fund salesman is selling mutual funds. I suggest that if you wish outside assistance, you engage the services of an individual or company that are not involved in marketing a product. In this manner, you will get unbiased advice. Many public accounting firms have established personal financial planning sections in their company that can be of assistance and will provide unbiased recommendations. However, regardless of who you engage as a consultant, you make the decisions. Don't let anyone tell you what to do. Have the individual present alternatives and perhaps his or her recommendations, but you make the decision. It's your money and it's your retirement.

An important part of financial planning is being certain that a proper will is in place. There must be a will for both you and your spouse. If you should die without a will, your assets would be distributed according to provincial intestacy law. This could be contrary to your wishes. In other words, your children and spouse might receive their fair share, but this may not be your wishes at the time of your death. The executors of your estate would be selected by the court, and your estate would be frozen immediately after your death until the court appointed the executors. Dying intestate would delay the distribution of your estate, resulting in higher administration costs. The will can contain certain provisions that would provide opportunities to defer or reduce income tax on death. This advantage would be lost.

Therefore, it is important that you and your spouse each have a will that leaves everything to the other upon death. This will result in minimal taxes. Without a will, your company is deemed to have been sold one minute before you died. It will be valued at that point and capital-gains taxes will be assessed accordingly. With a will that leaves everything to your spouse, there are no capital-gains taxes to be paid until his or her death.

Before closing this chapter on personal planning, it is

important to draw your attention to the consequences of the Family Law Act governing divorce. Some of the details vary from province to province. However, as a general statement, at the date of separation, both spouses will list their assets before they were married and at the date of separation. The increase will be divided equally between the two. In other words, if spouse one has a net increase of $100,000 and spouse two has a net increase of $50,000, then spouse one will give spouse two $25,000. The effect of this on small-business owners can be profound. For example, if you marry after you have started your business, then you should have a valuation performed at that time. I am not suggesting that everyone gets divorced, but the statistics indicate that about sixty percent of us will. At the date of separation, all your assets will be valued, including the company. In general terms, you will have a valuator perform a valuation of the shares of your company as will your spouse. The odds are, yours is lower and negotiations will take place in order to establish an acceptable value. Let us assume that you are number one spouse and your business is valued at $1,000,000. If the family home is worth $500,000, then your settlement may be to leave spouse two with the house and pay him or her $250,000 as the final settlement. The next question is: Where does the $250,000 come from? All you have is your company. These settlements in some cases can put a small-business owner in a tremendous cash bind.

Your spouse effectively owns fifty percent of your company. You may have trouble obtaining the necessary financing for the business without getting your spouse to cosign any of the bank loans. In other words, the bank realizes that in the event of your separation or divorce, half of the business really belongs to your spouse.

The ultimate solution, of course, is to obtain a marriage contract at the date of marriage whereby you opt out your small business from the matrimonial assets. If this is done, it virtually eliminates the problems set out above and makes it easier for future financing with the bank. If you have children who will be coming into the business, then it is recommended that they too have a family contract that will opt out the business from the matrimonial assets.

Personal financial planning and personal tax planning are very intricate parts of running your small business. No doubt, your ultimate goal is to maintain the lifestyle of your choice before retirement and be able to continue that lifestyle during retirement. Planning is the key.

15

GOAL REASSESSMENT: GROWING THE BUSINESS

Before you bought yourself a job, you established your personal goals. Probably this was the main reason for getting into your own business. At that time, you took a hard look at yourself to determine what you really wanted to be doing. You established the future lifestyle you wished to pursue and the corresponding financial requirements. Well, times change and so can your personal goals. Your sights might be aimed much higher than they were in the initial stages. Consequently, it is now time to take another hard look at yourself to determine where you want to be in five to ten years. New information and your current experiences will spearhead the results of your updated goals. The markets will change and new opportunities will become apparent.

In my case, I discovered after being in business for about six months that my business goal had to change. My original concept was to be the part-time controller for six or seven small-business owners, work out of my house, and have no employees. I quickly realized that I would only get paid when I worked. There were only so many hours in a day or a year. My total income was therefore "capped" with really no potential increase other than to raise my hourly rate charged to my clients. I also realized that my small-business clients could only afford so much. It was necessary to reassess my business goals. I also discovered that most of my clients did not have adequate information to allow me to be a good controller. So, an obvious expansion was to set up a bookkeeping service. Within four years, I had a thriving bookkeeping practice together with my controllership services. Eight bookkeepers were providing me with the monthly financial statements for my clients.

Then I hit another crossroads. Another goal reassessment. My clients required auditing services and expert tax planning. Up to this point, I referred this to one of the big eight accounting firms. My goal reassessment accelerated when I lost one of my good clients to this public accounting firm. In the next two years, three new partners joined the business to head up the income tax planning, auditing and accounting services and assist me in the controllership area. At the time of writing this book, there are seven partners. Our present ten-year plan is to expand the business and take on additional younger partners who will eventually provide for the succession of the four senior partners.

In this complex business world, I could never have developed the present accounting practice without having partners who had expertise in my weak areas.

It is important that every small-business owner take a hard look at his or her original personal and business goals. They should be updated in light of new information and changes in the business activity.

Consider the example of one small-business owner who had been in his own manufacturers' rep business for several years. On reassessing his goals, he realized that he was vulnerable. His manufacturing clients could cancel their agreement with him at any time and virtually eliminate all of his business. His solution was to purchase a small business whose products were compatible with his own knowledge. In this way, he was able to gain some control over his own destiny. He then proceeded, over the next fifteen years, to purchase several other companies on a planned basis, eventually reaching his ultimate goal, which was to "go public." You can now purchase shares in this small-business conglomerate on the Toronto Stock Exchange.

If he had not taken a hard look at his activity and reassessed his goals eighteen years ago, there is a good chance that he would still be a manufacturers' rep waiting for the axe to fall.

There is also the example of the small-business owner who was earning more than a reasonable living and was quite happy with his lot in life. I can remember discussing the possibility of improving the profits of his business by implementing certain inventory-control and information systems. At the time, the projected improvement was in the area of $50,000 to $100,000 per year. His response to the suggestion was Why? In other words: "I don't need the aggravation of managing my business in order to improve profits to earn money that I really don't feel I can spend." He had reviewed his personal and business goals and decided that the status quo was adequate.

In Chapter 13, we discussed the various stages in the life of a small business: start-up, development, growth, and consolidation. There is yet another stage, which we did not discuss. It's called the comfort stage.

Don't get me wrong. I am not critical of the small-business owner who decided to forego improved profits. At least he sat down and established his goals, which were to stand still. He was not interested in an expansion that might disrupt his current personal and business lifestyle. There is nothing wrong with that if that's what you want and as long as it is a conscious decision.

Another client, who was twenty-seven, had purchased a small business and run it successfully for four years. He reassessed his personal and business goals and decided to sell the business. He wanted to work for a bigger firm to expand his scope in the business world. Down the road, he would possibly come back and purchase another business when his appetite for general management in the big-business world was satisfied. His example perhaps shows that it is possible to start up or buy a business too soon. Remember that the majority of entrepreneurs are over thirty-five.

The message, then, is clear. Goal setting is a continual process, and your personal and business goals should be reexamined on a regular basis in light of new information, new trends, and revised personal lifestyle desires.

Strategic Planning

In addition to looking at your long-term personal goals, you must also continually engage in long-range business planning, sometimes referred to as strategic planning. To be a true entrepreneur and to be in control of your business, you must look down the road to evaluate the trends in your market area. For example, if you were in the courier business, you would have to evaluate the effect that FAX machines might have on your future growth, and determine the nature of your response.

The dynamic 1970s and 1980s have seen a tremendous swing from the manufacturing sector to the service sector. Automation, robotics, computer-assisted design (CAD), and computer-assisted manufacturing (CAM) have become the current buzz words for increased productivity and change. Some businesses have fallen by the wayside as a result of these dramatic changes; others have survived and expanded because of them.

Let's look at long-term survival planning. First, you must assess your product or service capabilities and get a handle on where your industry is going. It is important that you keep up to date on the newest developments in your industry and on the innovative products that are being developed so that you don't find yourself trying to market your industry's equivalent to the buggy whip.

Where do you find the crystal ball that will provide the answers for the future? Well, no crystal ball exists. You can, however, keep up to date by reading your trade publications, being active in your trade association, and by being on top of what is happening in your industry. This should be supplemented by reading national weekly financial newspapers and general business publications on a regular basis. By the way, when I say *read*, I really mean *skim*. Be a clipper. In other words, as trade magazines arrive on your desk, take two minutes to review the various articles and clip out those that appear appropriate and file them for future reading at a more convenient time. The use of a highlighter marking pencil can help emphasize some of the important items you wish to bring to your attention when you review the article.

Broaden your general business knowledge by attending management seminars, business conferences, and your trade association meetings and general discussions with colleagues in your industry. You must make time for this.

Keep an eye on the possibilities for diversification into completely different growth industries that can utilize your expertise and plant facilities. Although it is a general rule, confirmed by *In Search of Excellence*, to stick to your knitting, in some cases diversification may be advantageous to long-term survival. The market may be different. You may require some modification of your equipment. But it may provide you with a backstop, in case of difficult times in your present market area. In any event, if you stand still, the world will pass you by.

The faster the scene changes, the more important strategic planning becomes. Your firm's lifeline into the future depends on the plans that you make today. Obsolescence is commonplace and your long-term survival depends on your ability to plan years ahead. Granted, your long-term or strategic plan may prove not to be feasible at a future time. This means that your plans must be flexible.

If you look down the road and your personal goals and business goals suggest that you want to grow and expand and build your empire, then you may enter the realm of the medium-sized firm. This is a whole new ball game compared to a small business. The decision to grow or not to grow will require even more detailed planning and assessment of the requirements for future product lines, financing, personnel, and facilities.

Expansion

In a small business, the owner is able to be involved in many of the operation's day-to-day functions; in a medium-sized business, this involvement can be impossible. You will recall that, in Chapter 1, we recommended an exercise to help you measure your strengths and weaknesses. It is a good idea to redo this self-assessment to determine your current weaknesses.

You may have found that you are not entirely happy with your position in the company. Trying to cover the three areas of the tripod—marketing, operations, and finance—may be difficult for you. If your strengths lie in marketing and this is really what you like to do, then the future expansion will depend on you hiring the right senior people to cover the areas of your weakness. For example, there is no point hiring a strong marketing person when you really need a top financial individual to handle the finance leg of the tripod. Therefore, now is the time to determine what you really want to be doing in your own business. Plan to hire the appropriate individuals to cover the other areas of the management tripod.

All entrepreneurs must be both innovators and managers. But if you happen to be a stronger innovator than you are a manager, you will have to make some changes in your business's growth cycle.

Although innovation is an essential ingredient for long-term survival and for the progress and growth of a business, without good management the business is certain to flounder. Consequently, to grow your business and join the ranks of the medium-sized companies, you will need to hire people to manage the operations of your company. They will carry out the day-to-day supervision while you continue to dream up great new ways of increasing your market share, of developing new product lines, and generally expanding the sales and profits of your business.

Some innovator-entrepreneurs find this very difficult. For this new management team to be successful, an innovator-entrepreneur must allow the managers to manage. Daily interference is a no-no. However, there should be regular meetings to assess performance and to measure actual results against projections in the business plan. Monthly financial statements should be prepared showing the comparison between actual performance and the budget or plan that was set out at the first of the fiscal year. Any variances from the plan should be reviewed and, if necessary, the plan should be revised to reflect new information.

To the right innovator-entrepreneur, this phase of growing the business can be a lot of fun. The day-to-day niggly little problems, such as dealing with the bank, complaining customers, problem personnel, and so on, become the responsibilities of your managers. If you find this scenario appealing and if you're willing to give up the day-to-day, hands-on involvement, you probably will be around in the long term and will see your company grow beyond your original dreams.

In my view, the true entrepreneur is the person who has control and who is either a good manager himself or herself, or an innovator who recognizes the need for management assistance. The innovator-entrepreneur can become what I suggest is a true entrepreneur by compensating for his or her own weakness in the management area.

Internal Growth

Let's look at some of the factors to consider in your approach to internal growth. First, remember that bigger is not necessarily better. The plan for growth should be spearheaded by a view to increasing profits. In some cases, of course, expansion in one year may cause expenses to increase and profits to dip slightly. But the following year should have planned profits well in excess of the decreased profits in the current year. Too many small-business owners get caught up in what I refer to as the "numbers game." For example, in the first four years of operation, I had eight bookkeepers, a typist, a supervisor, and me (eleven people). The only question that any of my friends or colleagues ever asked was: "How many people are working for you?" It appeared that the barometer to measure the success of my business was the number of employees. No one asked me how much money I was making. As it turns out, at that point I had hit the consolidation stage and I probably had one bookkeeper too many. In today's dollars, that bookkeeper represented about $2,000 per month out of my back pocket. As I had monthly financial statements, it was apparent within two months that I was overstaffed, and corrective action was taken. However, it did cost me about $4,000 in today's dollars.

The secret to successful growth is planned and reasonable growth. Expanding too rapidly can cause a tremendous strain on your financing. The increase in accounts receivable and inventory will far outgrow the monthly profits. In addition, if the growth requires additional capital investment in fixed assets, your break-even point will increase substantially and you might find yourself on the razor's edge.

Another problem in rapid growth is that your customer

service may deteriorate. Your company was successful in the
first place because you provided effective customer service
on the way up. If you can't maintain this same effective quality of service to match your growth, you're heading for
trouble.

As you expand and proceed through any major growth
area, you must constantly review your personnel and their
skills. The skills required to run a business during this
dynamic period of expansion are different from those required
during the entrepreneurial start-up. This review of personnel can require some heart-rending decisions when you find
yourself either displacing or moving sideways some of your
old loyal faithful employees. However, if you have in the past
established an employee stock purchase plan, in which case
they own part of the business, then some of these individuals
will be pleased to see their investment increasing regardless
of the future employment they have with the company.

Then, too, another problem in expanding is your facilities.
Manufacturers may find themselves in a very difficult position if they haven't planned years ahead for this type of
expansion. If your plant is inadequate and there is no way
of increasing the space to handle the growth, then you will
be required to move. This can be costly, disruptive, and possibly set your company back in your expansion program.
Before the move, of course, strategic planning should take
place to determine your requirements for the next five to ten
years. I am not suggesting that you rent or build a plant
that would satisfy your growth position in ten years. However, you should keep uppermost in your mind the term *flexibility*. Flexibility is a big advantage for small-business
owners as they will be able to move very quickly when there
are changes in the trends in the marketplace. It is important that any new facilities have the flexibility to be
expanded as required.

Expansion and Financing: Can Venture Capitalists Help You?

A business plan should be prepared a minimum of once a
year, for the following year. This will include your forecast
monthly cash-flow statement and will indicate the financ-

ing required for your growing business. At some point, your financing needs may outgrow the services that your chartered bank is able to offer. You may find yourself looking to the venture capitalists for backing. A venture capitalist should only be approached if the chartered bank and your normal sources of financing are unable to meet the requirements of your expansion. We touched on this briefly in Chapter 6, but I think it is now time to give you some input as to how you should be dealing with the venture-capital firm.

Some people refer to venture capitalists as "vulture capitalists." I believe this to be a little unfair as these people, in most cases, are providing risk capital for a small business that is making the next step in its long-term expansion program.

Your business plan will indicate the cash requirements for the future expansion of your business. This plan, however, must be expanded to give the venture capitalist some idea of the growth and financial requirements for the next five years. This may sound impossible, but you are now in the big league and longer-term planning is necessary.

Before approaching venture-capital firms, you should obtain some basic information about each of them. Most venture-capital firms deal with specialized industries or special situations. For example, some only invest in high-tech projects; some only invest in mature medium-sized companies that require financing to help reorganize the share structure and possibly take out one of the current shareholders; some will not consider a venture-capital project under $1,000,000. In other words, investigate the venture-capital firms before you approach any of them to be certain that you are compatible with the company's operation. This research will save considerable time.

Once you have made a short list of three to five, then rank them, starting with the one that you feel is most compatible with your particular operation.

It is important that you understand where the venture capitalist is coming from. It has been suggested that many review 100 projects; invest in ten; and probably one of the ten is what they consider a winner (usually it goes public). Two are pretty good and the other seven fall into the categories of total losers and the living dead. Therefore, you are dealing with people who are willing to take the risks, but also are there to reap the rewards. This means that they want a piece of the action and they also expect to receive reasonable interest on the money advanced. In some cases, this takes the form of a convertible debenture with, say, a percent interest rate, and convertible at a per-share price established at the time of investment.

A convertible debenture is similar to a note payable or bond except that for each $1,000 of indebtedness, the debenture holder can convert to common shares on a formula basis. In other words, if a venture capital purchased $1,000,000 of convertible debentures in your company to finance expansion on the basis that this could be converted into 100,000 common shares, then the current value of the common shares is ten dollars per share. At a future time, if you wish either to take out the venture capitalist or go public, the shares could be worth over $20 per share. The venture capitalist, then, will receive a reasonable return of, say, 10% on the convertible debenture and obtain capital gain on conversion of the convertible debenture and sale of common shares of, say, 100% or more over a period of four years or more.

The investment objectives of the venture capitalist usually start at 25% per year, in addition to the return on his or her original investment at a reasonable interest rate. One thing you can be sure of: they will be betting on you as a top-flight manager. If your management team isn't sufficiently strong and fails to inspire sufficient confidence, you are not likely to be successful in obtaining the necessary venture capital.

Venture capitalists don't think like you. These people are not entrepreneurs. They are financial investors and are usually using other people's money, such as pension plans, personal consortia of individuals, and so forth. In addition to giving them a piece of your sweat equity, you will be required to put one or more of these people on the board. The individual(s) will monitor the progress of the investment on either a monthly or quarterly basis. This is good news and bad news. The good news is that you will have another string in your management bow. They will probably provide you with some management input that will assist in furthering the advancement of your business to higher profitability. The bad news is, of course, that some of this could be considered interference. As an old pro, you may have trouble accepting some of the theoretical comments and advice from young graduates of business schools.

If your ultimate goal is to take your company public, then the bridge from you, the entrepreneur, to the public market is assisted tremendously by the venture-capital route. Theoretically, your venture capitalist partners know the ropes. They should be able to direct you to optimize your personal position and theirs at the time of going public.

External Growth

Up to this point, we have been discussing growth from the inside. However, there is another approach that is much simpler, and faster, but possibly more costly. That is external growth; in other words, buying other businesses, either on a horizontal expansion or vertical integration. Horizontal expansion refers to buying out competitors; vertical refers to buying out suppliers and client companies. In some cases, it makes good business sense to purchase some suppliers who are critical to the future of your own business.

This does not preclude you from purchasing companies whose businesses are not associated with your prime products. However, if you move away from your "knitting," then you should be certain that the incumbent management stays on and assists you or your senior people in sustaining the successful operation of the acquisition. This was the strategy of the small-business owner whom I referred to earlier in this chapter whose company is now listed on the Toronto Stock Exchange.

While you proceed through the growth of your own business, you will become aware of other companies that you might consider purchasing as part of your long-term goals. In other words, you may have a key supplier whose owner is sixty-five years old and may wish to sell. Or you may have a major customer who is planning to retire.

In some cases, the customer or supplier whom you know to be a poor manager may have financial difficulties. You can possibly move in as a venture capitalist with the option to purchase all of the shares of the company. This can sometimes be considered bargain hunting. However, if one of your suppliers or customers is in receivership or is considered bankrupt, then my experience is that this can be dangerous and not necessarily a good deal.

Consider the example of the individual who was anxious to buy his own job and do it on the cheap. He purchased a small manufacturing concern that was currently in the hands of the bank's receiver. In his view, he would be able to get a really good deal. He made all the right moves: he developed a good business plan, acquired the necessary financing, hired key manufacturing personnel, and developed promotional literature. As he was a good salesman, he was able to get immediate orders to secure the success of his new business. Two of the three legs of the tripod—marketing and finance—were adequately covered. However, the major reason for the company going into receivership was that there was a problem with the equipment. The company was unable to produce economic quantities of the product. In six months, another receiver showed up. The message? Don't be too quick to grab a deal on the cheap.

Another approach to expanding or growing your business is to determine whether it is franchisable. You have now been running your business successfully for some years, have minimized or eliminated most of the problems, and possibly have what can be considered a package. There are many others who wish to buy themselves a job and may be interested in your type of business in a different location. One of the major advantages in expanding in this manner is that the capital required for inventory, fixed assets, and accounts receivable or other investments is minimized as it is provided by the franchisee. However, it is not simple to establish a franchise operation. You must first develop an operations manual setting out how you did it and how the franchisee can do it successfully. You can consider this similar to starting up a new business. You will be required to go through all of the basic steps of establishing a business plan, obtaining the necessary financing, and the market plan necessary to make your franchise successful.

In addition to selling the franchise, you will also be required to provide the support that you suggest is available as a result of payment for franchise fees. The upfront costs of establishing a franchise can be substantial, and the planning aspect is even more important than when you started in the first place. In most cases, you will charge an upfront franchise fee for the right to use any trademarks, for staff training, and so forth. You will also receive a percentage of sales as an ongoing fee for the support services. This may also include a percentage of sales for the national advertising. However, if you happen to be producing a product, then possibly you will obtain your ongoing franchise fee on the profit of the product being sold to your franchisee. It is fair to say that every franchise is different. Before you embark on this program, it is a good idea to discuss the details with existing franchisers that you may know to determine the pitfalls that lie ahead.

Another approach to expansion can be what is referred to as "branchising." This is similar to franchising, except that you really end up in partnership with the individual who is going to be your branch partner. There are many approaches to establishing how you might grow in this manner. One approach is the establishment of a new company in which the branch partner owns a minority interest, but provides the majority of the investment. In time, the branch partner is able to pick up for a predetermined amount an additional percentage to be a true fifty-fifty partner. In any event, consider this a true start-up, and take the necessary steps outlined previously in this book.

Part of your strategic plan should include how you wish to expand, whether internally or externally. It is important that you plan the financial resources very carefully. Don't expand yourself out of business.

Reassessing your personal and business goals is necessary on a regular basis. Life is short enough; too short to waste. If you are not happy with your work, then you are not happy with your life. If you find yourself losing interest in your current activities, then it is time to take a hard look at what is happening and where your new direction may be.